Biography

Gift of →

D1001839

GOD AND MYSELF

BY THE SAME AUTHOR

Mary: A History of Doctrine and Devotion
Adult Christianity
Mystics of Our Times
The Word of God in the World of Today
The Scholar and the Cross
The Light and the Rainbow
The Story of Mysticism

GOD AND MYSELF

The Spirituality of
JOHN HENRY NEWMAN

Hilda Graef

HAWTHORN BOOKS, INC.
Publishers New York

120706

Copyright © 1968 by Hilda Graef. Copyright under International and Pan-American Copyright Conventions. All rights reserved, including the right to reproduce this book, or portions thereof, in any form, except for the inclusion of brief quotations in a review. All inquiries should be addressed to Hawthorn Books, Inc., 70 Fifth Avenue, New York City 10011. Library of Congress Catalogue Card Number: 67-24651.

First American Edition: 1968

Printed in Great Britain

4450

BX
4705
N5
G74
1968

CONTENTS

		page
	Acknowledgments	7
	Preface	9
1	Early Developments	11
2	New Horizons	27
3	The Spirituality of the Oxford Movement	47
4	On His Way to the Catholic Church	79
5	'Spiritual Honeymoon'	101
6	Intellect and Spirituality	122
7	The Darkest Years	145
8	*The Apologia* and *The Dream of Gerontius*	157
9	Taking Stock of the Foundations	172
	Appendix: Newman on Lives of the Saints	183
	Bibliography	195
	Indices	199

ACKNOWLEDGMENTS

I wish to thank particularly Father
C. Stephen Dessain, of the Birmingham Oratory, for his unfailing encouragement and help with making
rare books and manuscript material
available to me, as well as Mr Derek
Priestley, of Peter Davies, for his
sustained interest and his valuable
suggestions.

Hilda Graef

NOTE

Throughout the text, parenthetical
comments by the author are indi-
cated by *square brackets*.

Comments in parenthesis by Newman himself in the quoted excerpts
from his writings are enclosed by
round brackets.

PREFACE

THOUGH much has been written on Newman and books and theses on him are still pouring from the presses both in the English-speaking countries and in Europe, hardly anything has been written on his spirituality. Yet Newman was one of the great spiritual teachers of the Church of England as well as of the Catholic Church, whose virile spirituality, nourished on the Scriptures and the Fathers of the Church, is perhaps more in tune with the twentieth than with the nineteenth century.

Why, then, the dearth of books on the subject? The reason seems to be that Newman's spirituality is scattered throughout his works and letters: one has to look for it in the eight volumes of the *Parochial and Plain Sermons*, in his *University Sermons*, his educational and philosophical works, in his diaries and retreat notes, and one has to read through volume after volume in order suddenly to find a page or even only a paragraph or a sentence that throws a bright light on his spirituality.

The modern reader should, however, be warned that he cannot expect a contemporary of Queen Victoria to teach the permissive morality of our own day, hence much of what he told his congregation at St Mary's, Oxford, may seem to us inordinately severe. This austere moral teaching must be understood in the context of his time; indeed it was a characteristic of the whole Oxford Movement whose leader Newman was, and that it made a deep impression on his contemporaries is evident from the enthusiastic reception of his sermons by his congregation as well as his readers.

Contrary to F. W. Faber and his friends at the Brompton Oratory in London, Newman did not think of himself as a spiritual teacher, since the London house had, so to speak, monopolized spirituality, leaving to Newman and his Birmingham Oratory scholarship and education. For this reason Newman's spirituality is not a separate department of his life and teaching, but integrated with both, hence his importance for our own world, which wants its spirituality applicable to ordinary Christians and not only to monks and nuns.

Oxford,
Lent 1967.   Hilda Graef.

1 EARLY DEVELOPMENTS

JOHN HENRY NEWMAN was born in London on February 21, 1801. His father was a banker, a member of the Church of England; his mother, to whom he was very devoted, was descended from a Huguenot family. John Henry was the eldest of six children, three boys and three girls. Both parents followed the ordinary practice of the established Church in the early nineteenth century, which Newman himself was later to do so much to change. This meant that the family went to church twice on a Sunday, to Matins and Evensong according to the Book of Common Prayer; there were daily morning and evening prayers, and Bible reading and the recitation of the Psalms were encouraged. Holy Communion was received only rarely. 'Of course,' as Newman himself writes in the *Apologia*, 'I had a perfect knowledge of my Catechism.'

Even as a small boy, John Henry had an intense interior life: 'I thought life might be a dream, or I an Angel and all this world a deception, my fellow-angels by a playful device concealing themselves from me, and deceiving me with the semblance of a material world.' Now many small children have the gift of 'seeing' things in their imagination, such as angels or strange countries. But this is not exactly what this passage means. It is precisely that John Henry did *not* see angels, but that he was aware of them without seeing them, for they were 'concealing themselves' from him, and he himself was one of them, while the surrounding material world seemed to him unreal, a kind of 'veil of Maya' as Indian philosophy has it. Nor was this attitude merely a childish fancy. For though, in later life, Newman of course fully acknowledged the reality of the material world, it nevertheless remained

11

for him a secondary reality, concealing the 'invisible world' of God and his spiritual creation.

Again in his *Apologia* he mentions a strange childhood practice of his. He was, he says, 'very superstitious, and . . . used constantly to cross myself on going into the dark'. Now for a Protestant boy to cross himself was surely very unusual, to say the least, and Newman himself could give no explanation for this, though he might of course have seen somebody crossing himself without being conscious of it, as there were some Catholic ladies in his village and two Catholic boys in his school.

When, many years later, he went through some old papers of his he found a copybook in which he had written some verses when he was not quite ten years old. There he came across 'a device which almost took my breath away with surprise'. He had drawn a large cross by the side of which was a kind of necklace with a small cross attached, obviously a set of Rosary beads. He comments in the *Apologia* that he probably got the idea from some romance or religious picture, 'but', he continues, 'the strange thing is, how, among the thousand objects which meet a boy's eyes, these in particular should so have fixed themselves in my mind, that I made them thus practically my own'. It is, indeed, very strange, and perhaps it is not too fanciful to suggest that there was in these religious gestures and objects something responding to a deep need in Newman, overlaid by many other interests in the following years, but which made itself felt later when he was drawn both intellectually and spiritually to the Catholic Church.

In the early years of puberty, however, a change came over him. He read Paine's Tracts against the Old Testament, some of Hume's Essays and various French verses denying the immortality of the soul, and was deeply impressed by their plausibility. He no longer wanted to be religious, but he did want to be 'virtuous'; there was something in the idea of being religious that he did not like, nor did he understand what it meant to love God.

This tendency to unbelief, however, was checked almost as soon as it had begun to develop. In 1816, when he was fifteen, he came under the influence of a clergyman of evangelical leanings, Walter Mayers, who lent him books, 'all of the school of Calvin'. He at first rejected this influence, but in August of the same year he had a deep religious experience, which brought about such a change in him that he could write almost seventy years later: 'I should say that it is difficult to realize or imagine the identity of the boy before and after August 1816 . . . I can look back at the end of seventy years as if on another person.' This is how he describes this experience in the *Apologia* in connection with the doctrine of final perseverance: *

'I received it [the doctrine] at once, and believed that the inward conversion of which I was conscious (and of which I still am more certain that that I have hands and feet), would last into the next life, and that I was elected to eternal glory. I have no consciousness that this belief had any tendency whatever to lead me to be careless about pleasing God. I retained it till the age of twenty-one, when it gradually faded away; but I believe that it had some influence on my opinions, in the direction of those childish imaginations which I have already mentioned, viz. in isolating me from the objects which surrounded me, in confirming me in my mistrust of the reality of material phenomena, and making me rest in the thought of two and two only absolute and luminously self-evident beings, myself and my Creator.'

Here we are already at the heart of Newman's spirituality, for he came to his faith not by way of the scholastic proofs of the existence of God from causality or finality; he did not see God as the First Cause of all things or become convinced of his existence by the design inherent in creation. The visible world around him matters to Newman only in so far as it is the transparent garment of the invisible world, which comes to him in the existential experience of God and his own self, the 'two only absolute and luminously self-evident beings'. According to his own interpretation this was not, however, a typical evangelical conversion experience. For he wrote five years later, in 1821, that he could

* The Calvinist teaching that the elect had the assurance that they would never fall away from God.

speak of conversion only 'with great diffidence, being obliged to
adopt the language of books. For my own feelings, as far as I
remember, were so different from any account I have ever read,
that I dare not go by what *may* be an individual case.' For the
classical evangelical conversion required a well-defined number
of stages, 'conviction of sin, terror, despair, news of the free
and full salvation, apprehension of Christ, sense of pardon, assurance of salvation . . . and so on to final perseverance', whereas
his own experience did not involve violent feelings, 'but a returning to, a renewing of, principles, under the power of the Holy
Spirit, which I had already felt, and in a measure acted on, when
young'.

Was it then a genuinely mystical experience? It is hard to say;
what tells against it is the fact that Newman says nothing of the
union between these two beings, God and himself, which is the
essence of a mystical experience; we might perhaps better call it
a philosophical experience, in some way akin to the Plotinian
'alone with the Alone', the human with the Divine spirit. What
gives it a Christian flavour, however, is the conviction that he
was 'elected to eternal glory'.

According to traditional Christian teaching no man can be
certain of his final salvation except by some extraordinary and
very rare private revelation. It seems, however, that this was not
the case with young Newman; his conviction of his own salvation
came to him probably under the influence of the Calvinistic books
he had read; for it is significant that, though his awareness of
God and himself remained with him throughout his life, the idea
that he was irrevocably destined to be saved left him when he was
twenty-one. At the moment, however, his experience caused him
to throw himself with all his energy into the practice of evangelical piety, which led him to minute self-observation and a Puritanical morality. In this year of his conversion the fifteen-year-old
boy wrote a poem which ended:

> O may I scorn each mundane joy,
> And meditate on Thee;

May heaven all my thoughts employ,
Then happy I shall be.

Towards the end of the same year he wrote a Latin prayer, in which he said he had earned eternal damnation because of his fearful crimes and asked God to save him from the attractions of the world such as parties and dances, which he condemns on the grounds that St Paul and St John have taught him to avoid the wicked joys of the world and to flee from the lust of the eyes, the lust of the flesh and the pride of life. He has therefore proposed to himself to fast and pray: 'May abstinence be my shield, may prayers be my sword.'

Such words from the pen of a very innocent, well-brought-up boy of fifteen may seem completely unreal to us today. But we have to remember that John Henry here imitated the language of the spiritual books he had been given by Mr Mayers, and these exaggerated self-accusations as well as a rather killjoy morality were the normal way in which a somewhat narrow Evangelicalism expressed itself. Nevertheless, to young Newman this language was quite real; his self-accusations were deeply felt and he religiously abstained from such 'sinful' pleasures as dances and any other activities he considered 'the beginnings of sin'. Among the authors he read at that time there was one, however, whose influence was so beneficial that Newman later wrote that, humanly speaking, he almost owed his soul to him. This was Thomas Scott (1747-1821), rector of Aston Sandford, whose writings gave him not only a deep understanding of the doctrine of the Holy Trinity, but also the conviction that faith alone does not save, but must be accompanied by good works. 'For years', Newman writes in his *Apologia*, 'I used almost as proverbs what I considered to be the scope and issue of his doctrine, *Holiness rather than peace,* and *Growth the evidence of life'*, two axioms that were later essential, the first as a principle of his preaching, and the second in his teaching on the development of doctrine.

His parents were none too pleased with his evangelical fervour, and John Henry was far too good a son to let his newly-found convictions upset the peace of the family. 'Although', he wrote, 'it is far from pleasant to give my reasons, inasmuch as I shall appear to set myself up, and to be condemning recreations and those who indulge in them, yet, when I am urged to give them, I hope I shall never be ashamed of them, presenting my scruples with humility and a due obedience to my parents, open to conviction, and ready to obey in a matter so dubious as this is, and to act against my own [judgement], if they command, thus satisfying at once my own conscience and them.' These words show a complete absence of fanaticism and obstinacy in his character that is rare in one so young and so sincere in his beliefs. Nor should it be assumed that these beliefs expressed themselves in a morose attitude to life that made his society unpleasant to his family. On the contrary, his younger brothers and sisters worshipped him, he and his mother were united by a most tender affection, and his chatty letters to his father prove how close was the relation between the two, though, as we shall see later, his father was by no means so uncritical of him as his mother and the younger members of the family.

Nor did John Henry's evangelical leanings prevent him from taking part in the ordinary recreations of his circle. He was an excellent violinist, and his letters to his family show that he could often be in a playful mood and had a great sense of humour. Thus in a letter to his father he gives his first impressions of Oxford, immediately after having been called into residence at Trinity College in June 1817. This austere young man told his father that 'the minute I had parted from you, I went straight to the tailor's, who assured me that, if he made me twenty gowns, they would fit me no better. . . .' He then describes his first dinner in hall, at which he 'was much entertained with the novelty of the thing. Fish, flesh and fowl,—beautiful salmon, haunches of mutton, lamb, etc., fine strong beer—served up in old pewter plates and misshapen earthenware jugs. Tell Mama there were gooseberry, raspberry, and apricot pies. . . . Tell Harriet [his sister] I have seen the fat cook. The wine has come; 8 per cent is taken off for ready money.'

This is surely not the letter of a gloomy Puritan averse to all worldly pleasures. On the other hand, he disliked the constant drinking by his fellow-undergraduates: 'They drank while I was there very much,' he writes, 'and I believe intended to drink again. They sat down with the avowed determination of each making himself drunk. I really think, if any one should ask me what qualifications were necessary for Trinity College, I should say there was only one, Drink, drink, drink.' So while John Henry appreciated the ordinary enjoyments of life, he disliked any excess; his studious and fastidious nature was averse to all debauchery, and he would never attend the annual 'Gaudy' of the college, when getting drunk was *de rigueur*. He wrote about this in 1819; 'Tomorrow is our Gaudy. If there be one time of the year, in which the glory of our College is humbled, and all appearance of goodness fades away, it is on Trinity Monday. O how the Angels must lament over a whole Society throwing off the allegiance and service of their Maker, which they have pledged the day before at His Table, and showing themselves true sons of Belial. It is sickening to see what I might call the apostasies of many. . . . The Gaudy has done more harm to the College than the whole year can compensate. An habitual negligence of the awfulness of the Holy Communion is introduced. How can we prosper?'

Here the narrowness of the young undergraduate's views is almost frightening. For surely getting drunk on one night and playing some pranks does not mean 'throwing off the allegiance and service' of God; one wonders what John Henry would have said of the Continental carnival before the beginning of Lent. He was even surprised that one of his friends 'was startled at the idea, when I said that . . . getting drunk, was, in the sight of God, nearly as great a crime as murder'. On the other hand, at that time he was not yet opposed to going to the theatre, even though he himself did so very rarely.

But there was one temptation that assailed him throughout his early university career, and which he took very seriously. His descriptions of it in his personal notes and his fight against it are

B

sometimes regarded by his critics as evidence of a repulsively puritanical outlook and even almost neurotic guilt complex. This was his ambition to do well in examinations. The expressions he used in his private notes on the subject are certainly exaggerated. In May 1818, when sitting for the Trinity College scholarship, 'I was sanguine that I should gain it, and I was fearful that I should be too much set upon it.' Therefore he prayed: 'O God of heaven and earth . . . let me not rely too much upon getting this scholarship. . . . So let me order my spirit, that, if I get it not, I may not be disappointed, but may praise and bless Thy name, as knowing better than myself what is good for me. O Lord God of hosts, grant it not to me, if it is likely to be a snare to me. . . .' He won the scholarship, and he thanked God, 'who only doth wondrous things. Give me grace, make me holy, for Thou alone canst'. Two years later, before taking his degree, when he read this prayer, he accused himself of being ungrateful: 'Could I be so lowly and resigned beforehand, so thankful on succeeding, and yet in a few short weeks become so vain, so puffed up, so proud, so quarrelsome, so very wicked?' He there-fore prays once more that God would not let him succeed with his degree 'if success would cause me to commit the least sin; I pray for grace to enable me to bear the event with thanksgiving and humility; and yet, yet, if I *am* successful, what may happen! May I not fall as before? is it not likely? what a heart is mine! . . . How probable then, since I have prayed the Lord that I may *not* succeed if sin must follow, how probable I shall fail!' Newman continues: 'O this spirit of mine, which keeps without inter-mission flattering me with the certainty of gaining honours, what need have I of resignation to the will of God! How disappointed without His mighty Spirit will be the proud soul within me!'

It may be said that this is all very exaggerated in a nineteen-year-old. Every student wants to do well in his examinations, indeed it is his duty to make every effort to give the best he can —why then all this fuss?

Four years before John Henry had written to Walter Mayers

that he had 'hidden faults', and the prayers just quoted show that he evidently considered that he had an inordinate ambition. It is the 'sins of the flesh' which are not only the most obvious, but against which young people are warned—or at least used to be warned!—most frequently. Newman seems scarcely to have been afflicted by them; indeed, he had had the conviction that God wanted him to be a celibate ever since his conversion at the age of fifteen. But the temptations of the flesh are not necessarily the most dangerous. There are temptations of the spirit, an inordinate longing for fame, for surpassing everyone else in one's work, coupled with equally inordinate depressions if anything goes wrong, if one does not reach the top of the ladder. It seems that young Newman was aware that this pride was his chief personal temptation, and that, if indulged in, it might finally separate him from God. For the sins of the spirit can do this even more effectively than the sins of the flesh; and even in these early years John Henry had sufficient psychological insight to realize the dangers of his exceptional intellect as well as those of his keen sensitivity to both praise and blame. It is true that his expressions are out of proportion to the seriousness of his fault; but, as he himself realized later, this was due mainly to the style of the evangelical reading matter that he had absorbed.

His resignation to failure was put to the test when, instead of taking his degree with a double First, as was expected by all his friends and tutors, in November 1820 he just passed 'under-the-line', as it was then called, corresponding to a third or fourth class according to the present system.

This failure was due to a complete breakdown caused by over-work—he had been steadily reading for an average of twelve hours a day, sometimes even more—and aggravated by what seems to have been insufficient tuition. But as John Henry had prayed for failure if success should cause him to sin, he took his misfortune with extraordinary calm, his chief concern being the disappointment of his parents. He did not, however, give up hope of a university career, though he abandoned his former plan of becoming a barrister in order to follow his strong inclination for taking Holy Orders. For the moment, however, he spent his time pursuing subjects that interested him, for example mineralogy, chemistry and music, and especially mathematics 'on account of the general strength it imparts to the mind'—a large and varied curriculum, indeed, which furnished a background to his spirituality very different from that of traditional Catholic spiritual authors brought up in a restricted atmosphere of ascetical and scholastic theology.

Newman's religious views were still influenced by his Calvinistic reading and the thoroughly fundamentalist interpretation of the Bible prevalent at the time among Christians of all denominations. He tried, for example, to answer objections to the Deluge by supposing that the Antediluvians were drowned in what are now the Indian and Pacific Oceans, and to give reasons for the Mosaic teaching on the age of the earth (c. 6,000 years) from contemporary geological findings. His awareness of the invisible world was further strengthened by a dream, in which, as he writes in his journal of June 1821, 'a spirit came to me, and discoursed about the other world. I had several meetings with it. . . . Among other things it said that it was absolutely impossible for the reason of man to understand the mystery (I think) of the Holy Trinity, and in vain to argue about it; but that every thing in another world was so *very, very plain*, that there was not the slightest difficulty about it. I cannot put into any sufficiently strong form of words the ideas which were conveyed to me. I thought I instantly fell on my knees, overcome with gratitude to God for so kind a message.'

Two months later he determined to go to Holy Communion with his brother Francis once a fortnight in the long vacation, a decision which his mother considered as 'righteous overmuch, and was verging upon enthusiasm'—'enthusiasm' being then regarded in the Church of England as one of the worst faults of a Christian. To prepare himself for the worthy reception of the sacrament Newman bought a book by which to examine his conscience, and the self-accusations that fill the pages of his diary show the artificiality of such a procedure : 'I find my pride, vanity, haughtiness, know no bounds. . . . I have been sadly deficient in meekness, long suffering, patience, and filial obedience. . . . I have many times fed my pride and vanity upon empty imaginations of my own importance. . . . As to ill temper, hastiness of spirit, cruelty, harshness of speech, I have not advanced an inch. . . . I have gone on day after day so grievously sinning in ill temper. . . . I have such dreadfully vain thoughts, am so conceited, and am becoming so self-dependent, that I have resolved through God's grace not to allow any thoughts to arise in my mind about any excellence I seem to myself to possess.'

Most of these self-accusations refer to sins of thought, and all of them are the typical imperfections of the young intellectual who finds it difficult to suffer fools gladly and cannot help being aware of his own superiority. On the other hand, this constant introspection, the fear of sinning by what was, after all, only the healthy ambition of an extraordinarily gifted young man, the scruples over every word and thought this self-examination induced led young Newman to a state of mind that alarmed his father, who, one day after church, spoke very seriously to him. 'Take care,' he warned. 'It is very proper to quote Scripture, but you poured out texts in such quantities. Have a guard. You are encouraging a nervousness and morbid sensibility, and irritability, which may be very serious . . . it is a disease of mind. Religion, when carried too far, induces a softness of mind. You must *exert* yourself and do every thing you can. Depend upon it, no one's principles can be established at twenty. Your opinions in two or three years will certainly, *certainly* change. . . . You are on dangerous ground. The temper you are encouraging may lead to something alarming. Weak minds are carried into superstition, and strong ones into infidelity. Do not commit yourself. Do nothing ultra. . . . I know you write for the *Christian Observer* [a fanatically Evangelical publication]. My opinion of the *Christian Observer* is this, that it is a humbug. . . . The letter was more like the composition of an old man, than of a youth just entering life with energy and aspirations.'

John Henry was impressed. He straightaway prayed 'earnestly

against any delusive heat or fanatic fancy . . . or uncharitable zeal'. Yet having decided to become a clergyman, his moral views became stricter than ever.]In the Christmas Vacation 1821 he had gone to the theatre once or twice; but then he read W. Wilberforce's *Practical Christianity*, 'a most delightful book', which determined him henceforth to avoid going to a play. During the summer holidays he prayed that 'when absent from home, we might have faithful preachers of His word, wherever we went'. He considered it a sin to write a letter on Sunday, a view which greatly annoyed his father.

But for all that, his scholarly ambitions refused to be suppressed. A few months after his disappointing degree examination he decided to stand for a Fellowship at Oriel College, one of the most coveted prizes of an academic career at Oxford. But again there was the interior struggle between his natural ambition and hopes and his fear that these might estrange him from God. Immediately after calling on the Provost of Oriel to ask permission to stand for the forthcoming election he writes: 'Hope will arise, do what I will; but it is instantly beaten down by some very weighty reflections. 1. I am not humble or spiritual enough to bear success yet. 2. It will make me too independent in money matters. . . . I am perpetually praying to get into Oriel. . . . O Lord, dispose of me as will best promote Thy glory—and, after that, as will best advance my sanctification—but give me resignation and contentment.' A day before the examination, on Easter Sunday, he received Holy Communion and wrote: 'I fear I am sadly attached to the world, for I am very much cast down and harassed by this Oriel business—but not so much perhaps from fear of failing, as from mortification at having given the Fellows a bad opinion of me by some careless blunders.'

This sensitivity to the opinion of others, which he was later to castigate severely in his sermons, was a characteristic that remained with him throughout the greater part of his life; it was the reverse side of his gift for friendship and the attraction he exercised on others. He confessed that after his first University Sermon in July 1826, for example, 'I lay on my sofa writhing, at the thought what a fool I had made of myself.' His fears about the Oriel examination, however, proved groundless, and on April 12, 1822 there is only one short entry in his diary: 'I have this morning been elected Fellow of Oriel. Thank God, thank God.'

The election to the fellowship of Oriel did not only decisively affect his worldly position, it also gradually brought about a profound change in his religious views. For the atmosphere in the Oriel Common Room was anything but evangelical; John Keble was High Church and John Whately, later Anglican Archbishop of Dublin, was a keen logician as well as an active opponent of evangelicalism. From him Newman first learned 'the idea of the Christian Church, as a divine appointment, and as a substantive visible body, independent of the State, and endowed with rights, prerogatives and powers of its own'.

With the main object of his ambitions achieved—for he hoped to 'live and die a Fellow of Oriel', he now prayed: 'O save me from a useless life, keep me from burying my talent in the earth', even though he still accused himself from time to time of pride and overbearing behaviour. During his first years at Oriel his evangelicalism was still strong; he had pangs of conscience about dining with the Provost on Sunday and decided that he 'must explain myself in some way to the Fellows about my wish to keep Sunday holy'. His religion was based on the Bible as firmly as ever; indeed he now set himself to learn by heart large portions of it, for example in October 1823 he records having just finished the Epistle to the Hebrews, and a month later he had committed a large part of Isaiah to memory. When advising his sister Harriet to do the same he tells her that 'the benefit seems to me incalculable. It imbues the mind with good and holy thoughts. It is a resource in solitude, on a journey, and in a sleepless night; and let me press most earnestly upon you and my other dear sisters, as well as on myself, the frequent exhortations in Scripture to prayer'.

In his personal spiritual life he experienced the ups and downs that come to all who practise prayer regularly. On November 16,

1823 he writes: 'Received the Sacrament in chapel; but my thoughts wander, and my heart is cold—and I have just returned home sad. Yet this morning from 6 to 7 God granted me to pray fervently.' These vicissitudes became even more noticeable before his being ordained deacon, an event for which he prepared by prayer and fasting, with an earnestness (a favourite term of his) and a devotion rare in the Church of England of his days. On Friday, June 11, 1824, two days before, he wrote with great fervour: 'As the time approaches for my ordination, thank God, I feel more and more happy. Make me Thy instrument . . . make use of me, when Thou wilt, and dash me to pieces when Thou wilt. . . .' But the next day his mood had changed: 'Now, on returning home, how hard my heart is, how dead my faith. I seem to have an unwillingness to take the vows, a dread of so irreparable a step, a doubting whether the office is so blessed, the Christian religion so true.' But after the ceremony had actually taken place he writes: 'It is over. I am thine, O Lord; I seem quite dizzy, and cannot altogether believe and understand it. At first, after the hands were laid on me, my heart shuddered within me; the words 'for ever' are so terrible. It was hardly a godly feeling which made me feel melancholy at the idea of giving up all for God. . . . Yet, Lord, I ask not for comfort in comparison of sanctification. . . . I feel as a man thrown suddenly into deep water.' The opposition of comfort to sanctification was a thought he was later to develop in his sermons. How seriously he took his ministry, which to many of his contemporaries was no more than a career reserved particularly for the younger sons of good families, is clear from the entry in his diary the day after his ordination: ' "For ever", words never to be recalled. I have the responsibility of souls on me to the day of my death . . .' and he calls his ordination 'the time of my espousals', an expression that makes it clear that he gave it a truly mystical significance.

Shortly before his ordination he had accepted the curacy of St Clement's, a growing Oxford parish just beyond Magdalen Bridge. He was still under the influence of the evangelical doctrines he had learned at fifteen from Mr Mayers, and the authors Mayers had recommended. These rejected baptismal regeneration, and taught the necessity of a personal conversion experience and salvation by faith in the atoning death of Christ. Besides, they emphasized the sole authority of Scripture, while refusing the Church any right of a binding interpretation and stressed the importance of preaching to the detriment of liturgical worship. When the young curate discussed his first sermon with Edward Hawkins, then Vicar of St Mary's and later Provost of Oriel, he came up against unexpected criticism. Hawkins objected to an implicit denial of baptismal regeneration and to Newman's division of 'the Christian world into two classes, the one all darkness, the other all light', which simply did not correspond to the facts of experience, since most men were neither saints nor criminals but something in between. Such criticism had 'a great though a gradual effect' on Newman, enforced by books Hawkins gave him, so that he slowly came to be weaned of his evangelical opinions.

This, however, did not happen without a considerable struggle, reflected in his diaries. On August 15 he wrote: 'The question of regeneration perplexes me very much.' Ten days later his difficulties had increased: 'Lately I have been thinking much on the subject of grace, regeneration etc. . . . I am always slow in deciding a question; last night I was so distressed and low about it, that a slight roughness from someone nearly brought me to tears, and the thought even struck me I must leave the Church. I have been praying about it before I rose this morning, and I do not know what will be the end of it. I think I really desire the truth, and would embrace it wherever I found it.'

His uncertainties were aggravated by the fact that some of his friends were Calvinists and tried to pull him in the opposite direction, so that he cried out: 'What shall I do? I really desire the truth.'

The problem was driven from his mind for a few weeks by the illness and death of his father. Newman had never seen a dead body before; the sight confirmed him in his belief in the unseen

world: 'Can a man be a materialist who sees a dead body?' he
asked. After his father's death his thoughts turned to his own
future. 'When I die, shall I be followed to the grave by my children,' he asked himself. 'My mother said the other day,' he continues, 'she hoped to live to see me married, but *I* think I shall
either die within a College walls, or a Missionary in a foreign land
—no matter where, so that I die in Christ.' His prediction was not
far wrong.

2 NEW HORIZONS

AFTER his father's death Newman returned to Oxford and resumed his discussions about the theological problems that continued to agitate him. He would often work them out in arguments with E. B. Pusey, at that time also a Fellow of Oriel, 'I arguing for imputed righteousness*, he against it, I inclining to separate regeneration from baptism, he doubting its separation, etc.' By January 1825 he had come to the tentative conclusion that he must give up the doctrine of imputed righteousness and that of regeneration as apart from baptism, and his experience in the parish confirmed him in his change of views, because, as he writes in July 1825, about two months after he had been ordained priest: '. . . in my parochial duties I found many, who in most important points were inconsistent, but whom yet I could not say were altogether without grace. Most indeed were in that condition as if they had some spiritual feelings, but weak and uncertain.'

Besides, Newman's cast of mind and his interests were far too comprehensive to allow a narrow evangelicalism a more than temporary hold on him. For from his earliest years he had been attracted to the classics; he delighted in Aeschylus and Pindar, Virgil and Horace, Aristotle and Cicero. In 1823 he had already drawn up an argument for strict Sunday observance from the fourth century Greek Father St John Chrysostom; thus his scruples in this direction were due as much to Patristic teaching as to his evangelical outlook. Gradually, his views became more liberal; for as early as February 1825 he wrote in his journal: 'As to the

---

* i.e. the Lutheran view that the righteousness of Christ is only imputed to a man without making him righteous in himself, summed up in Luther's words: *simul iustus et peccator*, viz. a just man at the same time as a sinner.

observance of the Sabbath, I confess I waver very much, but to a
clergyman, whose hands are full of business on Sunday it is personally a question of comparatively small importance.'

He was not only 'full of business' on Sundays. In 1825 besides
having to raise funds for a new church at St Clement's he became
Vice-Principal of Alban Hall and in the next year wrote his *Essay
on Miracles*, in which he defended the Biblical miracles, including
such as Joshua making the sun stand still, but rejected all the
miracles reported in the early Church and, with particular venom,
the 'Popish miracles' of the Catholic saints. On his twenty-fifth
birthday (February 21, 1826) he took stock of his spiritual and
theological development. 'I have been very vain this year, inordinately vain of my acuteness, clearness of mind and despising others
. . . I fear thoughts of theological fame, desire of rising in the
Church.' On the other hand he stated an improvement 'in judgement of late, being more cautious, less fanciful'. He had become
far less Calvinistic in his views, so much so that Pusey accused
him of becoming High Church.* In 1826, he had also just been
appointed one of the public Tutors of his college, and had con-
sequently given up the vice-principalship of Alban Hall as well
as the curacy of St Clement's. Entering upon his new duties he
wrote in his journal: 'May I engage in them in the strength of
Christ, remembering I am a minister of God, and have a commission to preach the gospel, remembering the worth of souls,
and that I shall have to answer for the opportunities given me
of benefiting those who are under my care,' and in a letter to his
mother: 'I have a great undertaking before me in the tutorship
here. I trust God may give me grace to undertake it in a proper
spirit, and to keep steadily in view that I have set myself apart
for His service for ever."

For Newman education was, and remained throughout his life,
a profoundly religious activity; it meant the spiritual as well as the

---

* Name that came into existence at the end of the seventeenth century, designating
a party in the Church of England emphasizing its Catholicity and episcopal authority,
but differing from the later nineteenth and twentieth century 'High Church' in laying
far less stress on ceremonial and being much more opposed to the Roman Catholic
Church.

intellectual formation of men. After his ordination he had written 'I have the responsibility of souls on me to the day of my death,' and this responsibility included everything. Indeed, before entering on his tutorial duties he had had some doubt whether these were compatible with his ordination vows; he had resolved it by taking the view that 'the Tutorial office was but another way, though not so heroic a way, as a mission to idolaters'. And in his playful poem 'Snapdragon', inspired by the plant that grew under his window in the college wall, he writes:

> Be it mine to set restraint
> On roving wish and selfish plaint. . . .
> Mine, the Unseen to display
> In the crowded public way,
> Where life's busy arts combine
> To shut out the Hand Divine. . . .
> May it be! then well might I
> In College cloister live and die.

This view of his tutorship, however, was not unchallenged, especially as he lost no time putting his strict religious views into practice. He objected to what he considered a profanation of Holy Communion, which the undergraduates attended once a term and which was sometimes followed by a champagne breakfast at which they would get drunk. Soon he had gathered a circle of young men whom he imbued with his own views. 'With such youths' he writes, 'he [that is himself] cultivated relations, not only of intimacy, but of friendship, and almost of equality, putting off, as much as might be, the martinet manner then in fashion with College Tutors, and seeking their society in outdoor exercise, on evenings, and in Vacation. And, when he became Vicar of St Mary's in 1828 the hold he had acquired over them led to their following him on to sacred ground, and receiving directly religious instruction from his sermons.'

Early in the same year (January 1828) an event had happened that intensified his awareness of the unseen world and strengthened his resistence to the liberalism surrounding him, which had shown signs of weakening. This event was the sudden death of his much-loved sister Mary. Four months later he wrote about her to his sister Jemima: 'Dear Mary seems embodied in every tree and hid behind every hill. What a veil and curtain this world of sense is! beautiful, but still a veil.' The reality behind the veil was the invisible world of God and his angels, which was at the centre of his spirituality. About the same time he expressed the deep impression made by this death in a poem called 'Consolations in Bereavement', of which we will quote the first and the last stanza:

> Death was full urgent with thee, Sister dear,
>   and startling in his speed;—
> Brief pain, then languor till thy end came near—
>   Such was the path decreed,
>   The hurried road
> To lead thy soul from earth to thine own God's abode.
>
> Joy of sad hearts, and light of downcast eyes!
>   Dearest thou art enshrined
> In all thy fragrance in our memories;
>   For we must ever find
>   Bare thought of thee
> Freshen this weary life, while weary life shall be.

If the death of his sister turned Newman's mind again to the unseen world, new influences led him in a direction increasingly opposed to narrow evangelicalism. In the long vocation he began to read the Fathers systematically, beginning with the second century Apostolic Fathers such as St Ignatius of Antioch and the 'apologist' Justin Martyr. About the same time Hurrell Froude, the son of Archdeacon Froude, had been elected Fellow of Oriel, together with Robert Wilberforce, the second son of William Wilberforce, the famous advocate of the abolition of slavery. Froude became one of Newman's most intimate friends, and his religious views, which were diametrically opposed to those of Walter Mayers and the evangelical authors he had recommended, could not fail to open new vistas to Newman, even though he was certainly not swept off his feet, as is clear from a very revealing passage in the *Apologia*; 'He [Hurrell Froude] professed openly his admiration of the Church of Rome, and his hatred of the Reformers. He delighted in the notion of an hierarchical system, of sacerdotal power, and of full ecclesiastical liberty. He felt scorn of the maxim, 'The Bible and the Bible only is the religion of Protestants', and he gloried in accepting Tradition as a main instrument of religious teaching. He had a high severe idea of the intrinsic excellence of Virginity; and he considered the Blessed Virgin its great Pattern . . . he had a vivid appreciation of the idea of sanctity, its possibility and its heights; and he was more than inclined to believe a large amount of miraculous interference as occurring in the early and middle ages. He embraced the principle of penance and mortification. He had a deep devotion to the Real Presence, in which he had a firm faith. He was powerfully drawn to the Medieval Church, but not to the Primitive. . . . He had no turn for theology as such. He set no sufficient value on the writings of the Fathers. . . .' Newman himself admitted that it was 'difficult to enumerate the precise additions to my theological creed which I derived from a friend to whom I owe so much. He taught me to look with admiration towards the Church of Rome, and in the same degree to dislike the Reformation. He fixed deep in me the idea of devotion to the Blessed Virgin, and he led me gradually to believe in the Real Presence.' But he never instilled in his friend his own love of the medieval Church; Newman remained throughout his life firmly attached to the teaching of the early Fathers. These also supported him in his religious view of his tutorial office, for he quotes Origen as well as William Laud's statutes for Oxford for the opinion which 'he held almost fiercely that secular education could be so conducted as to become a pastoral cure'. When it became impossible to continue his tutorship in this spirit he finally gave it up (1832), for he felt intensely that 'unless he could make his educational engagements a fulfilment of his ordination vow, he could have no part in them'.

In 1829 the way in which the government handled the Emancipation of Roman Catholics from the disabilities which had been

imposed on them for centuries upset Newman deeply. He would
not have opposed Catholic Emancipation itself; but he resented
its being treated merely as a matter of political expediency as
evidence of the complete religious indifference of the government.
For Robert Peel, Conservative Member for the University of Oxford, had originally been against Catholic Emancipation; but when
he realized that the alternative could only be civil war in Ireland
he introduced the Emancipation Bill in Parliament. After such
a complete volte face, however, Peel felt constrained to test the
confidence of his electors; hence he resigned in order to stand
again. This caused a by-election in Oxford, in which Newman
took a very active part. The majority of the members of the Oriel
Common Room, including Pusey, were in favour of re-electing
Peel, while Newman fought desperately against it. His party
gained a victory; Peel was defeated. Why had the retiring scholar
suddenly become so violent a partisan in politics?

The explanations he gives in two letters to his mother, who was
very puzzled by her son's activities, show that the underlying
reasons, though imperfectly expressed, were spiritual. On March
1, 1829, in the first flush of victory, he writes: 'We have achieved
a glorious victory. It is the first public event I have been concerned
in, and I thank God from my heart both for my cause and its
success. We have proved the independence of the Church and of
Oxford . . . They [the supporters of Peel] strutted about (pea-
cocks!) telling our men who passed through London that they
should beat [us] by eight to one, and they wondered we should
bring the matter to a poll. We endured all this, scarcely hoping for
success, but determining, as good Churchmen and true, to fight
for the *principle*, not consenting to our own degradation. . . .
Well, the poor defenceless Church has borne the brunt of it, and
I see in it the strength and unity of Churchmen. An hostile
account in one of the papers says, "High and Low Church have
joined, being set on rejecting Mr Peel".'

Not quite a fortnight later, in the second letter, on March 13,
he develops his thought still further, pointing out the dangers to
the Church and Christianity in general from the increasing liberal-

ism of the times, linking again religion and education: 'We live
in a novel era,' he writes, 'one in which there is an advance to
universal education. Men have hitherto depended on others, and
especially on the clergy, for religious truth; now each man attempts
to judge for himself. Now, without meaning of course that Christianity is in itself opposed to free inquiry, still I think it *in fact* at
the present time opposed to the particular form which that liberty
of thought has now assumed. Christianity is of faith, modesty,
lowliness, subordination; but the spirit at work against it is one
of latitudinarianism, indifferentism, and schism, a spirit which
tends to overthrow doctrine, as the fruit of bigotry and discipline
—as if the instrument of priestcraft. All parties seem to acknowledge that the stream of opinion is setting against the Church. . . .
Yet I do still think there is a promise of preservation to the Church;
and in its Sacraments, preceding and attending religious education, there are such means of Heavenly grace, that I do not doubt
it will live on in the most irreligious and atheistical times. . . .
And now I come to another phenomenon: the talent of the day
is against the Church. The Church party (visibly at least, for there
may be latent talent, and great times give birth to great men) is
poor in mental endowments. It has not activity, shrewdness, dex-
terity, eloquence, practical power. On what, then, does it depend?
On prejudice and bigotry.

'This is hardly an exaggeration; yet I have good meaning and
one honourable to the Church. Listen to my theory. As each individual has certain instincts of right and wrong antecedently to
reasoning, on which he acts . . . so, I think, has the world of
men collectively. God gave them truths in His miraculous revelations, and other truths in the unsophisticated infancy of nations,
scarcely less necessary and divine. These are transmitted as "the
wisdom of our ancestors", through men—many of whom cannot
enter into them, or receive them themselves— still on, on, from
age to age, not the less truths because many of the generations
through which they are transmitted are unable to prove them, but
hold them, either from pious and honest feeling . . . or from
bigotry or from prejudice. That they are truths it is most difficult

to prove, for great men alone can prove great ideas or grasp them.
. . . Moral truth is gained by patient study, by calm reflection,
silently as the dew falls—unless miraculously given—and when
gained it is transmitted by faith and by "prejudice".'

Here Newman discussed three problems of the Christian life
which are still with us more than a century later: the impact of
general education, liberty of thought, and the fact—even more
noticeable in his time than it is now—that the anti-Christian
elements are far superior in intellect and energy. The fundamental
Christian virtues, as he sees them, are opposed to 'free inquiry';
faith rests on dogmatic statements which in their turn require the
submission of the intellect to what it cannot itself fully comprehend, while the modern liberal intellectual refuses to submit
his mind to anything that would limit his freedom, even if it
comes to him with the authority of divine revelations. But for
Newman reasoning is not the basic activity by which man finds
truth; for even in the sphere of 'natural' truths he must rely on
the findings of others, because only 'great men can prove great
ideas or grasp them'. This was a line of thought which he was to
develop later; it obviously came to him from the 'traditions' of the
Fathers of the Church, which had to be accepted by the ordinary
Christians who could not think out theological problems for
themselves.

Newman's work on the Fathers resulted in his first full-length
book, *The Arians of the Fourth Century* (1833), in which retreat
from evangelicalism was taken a step further. Though it is pro-
fessedly a doctrinal and historical work, it nevertheless contains a
certain amount of teaching that has a bearing on his spirituality.
Far from still holding that the Bible is the only rule of faith,
Newman now realized that it needed an authoritative interpretation, because the human mind is so constituted that it will reflect
on the object of its worship and thus may be led into error. For,
he says, 'Scripture being unsystematic, and the faith which it
propounds being scattered through its documents, and understood
only when they are viewed as a whole, the Creeds aim at con-
centrating its general spirit, so as to give security to the Church.'

But the creeds do not remove the mystery. Newman had always had a strong sense of mystery, and the teaching of the Fathers with its stress on the divine transcendence only increased it. However intellectual his approach, 'There,' he writes, 'the inquisitiveness of a pious mind rests, viz. when it has pursued the subject into the mystery which is its limit.' It was the mystery that the rationalizing Arians tried to avoid by denying Christ's perfect equality with God the Father, while Newman affirmed that 'a belief in our Lord's Divinity is closely connected . . . with deep religious feeling generally,—involving a sense both of our need and of the value of the blessings which He has procured for us, and an emancipation from the tyranny of the visible world,—it is not wonderful, that those, who would confine our knowledge of God to things seen, should dislike to hear of His true and only Image.' Here Newman now links up his profound realization of the unseen world with the Divinity of Christ. Far from explaining away the darkness of faith, the Church's creeds illuminate it by leaving the mystery intact, and the Son of God himself, by becoming Man, did not submit to the visible world, but freed us from its tyranny by giving us access to the invisible world in which He dwells. His study of the Fathers had convinced Newman that Christianity is inseparable from the Church, and that 'If the Church would be vigorous and influential, it must be decided and plain-spoken in its doctrine. . . . If the Church be the pillar and ground of the truth, and bound to contend for the preservation of the faith once delivered to it . . . then it is evidently our duty piously and cautiously to collect the sense of Scripture, and solemnly to promulgate it in such a form as is best suited . . . to exclude the pride and unbelief of the world.'

To prepare him for accomplishing this duty, Newman was now given what a modern psychologist (Ernst Kretschmer) has called 'the creative pause', a six months' interruption of his work during which a variety of new impressions and a severe illness combined to deepen his sense of his own vocation.

Since his tutorship had come to an end after a vehement controversy with his Provost, who objected to Newman's conception of a tutor as a spiritual guide, and as his book on the Arians was finished Newman agreed, after some heart-searching, to accompany his friend Hurrell Froude and his father on a Mediterranean cruise from which Hurrell hoped for an improvement in his lung trouble. The letters and poems written during this cruise throw much light on his spiritual state during these last months before the beginning of the Oxford Movement.

One of the most innocent enjoyments as it would seem, and one that would easily lead a man to the worship of his Creator, is the enjoyment of the beauties of nature. A Catholic mystic like St Teresa of Avila, for example, wanted her convents built with beautiful views, so that her nuns, deprived of most of the ordinary comforts of life, should at least take some pleasure in God's creation. But for Newman natural beauty had a magic that frightened him. How sensitive he was to it is shown by many descriptions in his letters; for example in one to his mother, from Dartington (July 1831) he wrote: 'What strikes me most is the strange richness of everything. The rocks blush into every variety of colour, the trees and fields are emeralds, and the cottages are rubies. The beetle I picked up at Torquay was as green and gold as the stone it lay upon. . . . The scents are extremely fine, so very delicate and powerful, and the colours of the flowers as if they were all shot with white. The sweet peas especially have the complexion of a beautiful face. . . . Let me enjoy what I feel. . . .' But a few days afterwards he wrote a poem, called *The Pilgrim*: in a very different strain:

> There stray'd awhile, amid the woods of Dart,
> One who could love them, but who durst not love.
> A vow had bound him, ne'er to give his heart
> To streamlet bright, or soft secluded grove.
> 'Twas a hard humbling task, onwards to move
> His easy-captured eyes from each fair spot,
> With unattach'd and lonely step to rove
> O'er happy meads, which soon its print forgot:—
> Yet kept he safe his pledge, prizing his pilgrim-lot.

If he felt the danger of giving his heart to the beauties of nature so strongly even in comparatively unexciting scenery, his reactions were intensified in the far more flamboyant atmosphere of the Mediterranean. Thus, after a brief visit to Gibraltar he wrote to his sister in December 1832: 'I no longer wonder at younger persons being carried away with travelling and corrupted; for certainly the illusions of the world's magic can hardly be fancied while one remains at home. I never felt any pleasure or danger from the common routine of pleasures, which most persons desire and suffer from—balls, or pleasure parties, or sights—but I think it does require strength of mind to keep the thoughts where they should be while the variety of strange sights—political, moral, and physical—are passed before the eyes, as in a tour like this.'

These words were not written in a passing mood; the next few days he wrote to his mother in a similar vein. After telling her that amongst the beautiful sights he would greatly have preferred to be back in Oxford, immersed in his usual occupations, he continues: 'For what are all these strange sights but vanities, attended too, as they ever must be, with anxious watchfulness lest the heart be corrupted by them.' Here again the evangelical views of his youth mingle with the austerity of the early Fathers for whom the beauties of the visible world were so many temptations of the devil. Besides, at thirty-one Newman had already become very settled in his habits as well as being so deeply attached to England and more especially to Oxford that any break with his normal life was irksome rather than pleasurable. In March 1833 he wrote to his friend Frederic Rogers from Rome: 'I long to be back, yet wish to make the most of being out of England, for I never wish to leave it again,' and a few days later he wrote to another friend: 'I never loved home so well as now I am away from it—and the exquisite sights which foreign countries supply both to the imagination and the moral taste are most pleasurable in *memory*, but scarcely satisfactory as a present enjoyment. There is far too much of tumult in seeing the places one has read so much about all one's life, to make it desirable for it to continue. I did not know

before, the mind could be excited in so many various ways; but
it is as much so as if it were literally pulled about, and had now
a leg twitched and now one's head turned.'

With such an attitude it is hardly surprising that Newman
should confess that he had experienced 'none of that largeness and
expansion of mind which one of my friends privately told me I
should get from travelling'. For the fact is that Newman's essential life was lived in the invisible world, and for this reason the
quickly changing impressions of new places were only a distraction
of this intense inner life which needed the intellectual routine of
the quiet existence of the scholar for its vigour and expansion.
An extrovert poet like Goethe, for example, found in the beauties
and experiences of Italy the matter necessary for the full development of his gifts; while for an inward-looking contemplative like
Newman they were no more than interruptions with hardly any
effect on the evolution of his mind.

The very titles of his poems which he poured out in profusion
throughout his voyage are significant. To give but a few examples:
Private Judgement, Absolution, Memory (beginning, characteristically: 'My home is now a thousand miles away'), *England,
Moses, Abraham, Temptation, Liberalism*—certainly not subjects
one would expect to inspire a poet who sees Corfu, Messina, Val-
letta for the first time.

At the beginning of March 1833 Newman and his party arrived
in Rome; and the letters and poems he wrote while there show
the extraordinary attraction, mingled with disgust, a kind of love-
hate which he developed for this centre of Christianity. On March
4, two days after his arrival, he wrote to his sister Harriet: 'And
now what can I say of Rome, but that it is the first of cities, and
that all I ever saw are but as dust (even dear Oxford inclusive) compared with its majesty and glory? Is it possible that so serene and
lofty a place is the cage of unclean creatures? I will not believe
it till I have evidence of it. In St Peter's yesterday, in St John
Lateran today, I have felt quite abashed, chiefly by their enormous
size, added to the extreme accuracy and grace of their proportions,
which make one feel little and contemptible.' How very much

Newman was at that time in two minds about Rome is shown
in a letter to a friend a few days later: '. . . you have to view
Rome as a place of religion; and here what mingled feelings come
upon one—you are in the place of martyrdom and burial of
apostles and saints; you have about you the buildings and the
sights they saw, and you are in the city to which England owes the
blessing of the Gospel. But then, on the other hand, the super-
stitions, or rather, what is far worse, the solemn reception of them
as an essential part of Christianity. But then, again, the extreme
beauty and costliness of the churches; and then, on the contrary,
the knowledge that the most famous [St Peter's] was built
(in part) by the sale of indulgences. Really this is a cruel place. . . .
It is a mine of all sorts of excellences.'

Rome was, indeed, cruel to him; for on the one hand he felt
its immense attraction, on the other all he had ever been taught
about it was that its doctrines and worship were perverted. These
strangely mixed feelings found their most moving expression in a
poem he wrote a few months later in Palermo:

> Oh that thy creed were sound!
> For thou dost soothe the heart, thou Church of Rome,
> By thy unwearied watch and varied round
> Of service, in thy Saviour's holy home.
> I cannot walk the city's sultry streets,
> But the wide porch invites to still retreats,
> Where passion's thirst is calm'd, and care's unthankful gloom.
>
> There, on a foreign shore,
> The home-sick solitary finds a friend:
> Thoughts, prison'd long for lack of speech, outpour
> Their tears; and doubts in resignation end.
> I almost fainted from the long delay
> That tangles me within this languid bay,
> When comes a foe, my wounds with oil and wine to tend.

He still regarded her as a foe, the Church of Rome—yet she

soothed his heart; in the dark churches of Palermo the wearied traveller found a peace the source of which he as yet could not comprehend; the Catholic Church seemed to him like the good Samaritan, 'unorthodox' in creed, yet soothing in her ministrations even to one who did not belong to her. Perhaps this very attraction he had felt in Italy partly accounted for the violence with which Newman was soon to attack her.]

He had arrived quite worn out in Palermo after a very serious illness—most probably typhoid fever—which he considered throughout his life to have had a profound spiritual significance for him. He has left a very detailed account both of his physical and his spiritual state during these painful weeks in Sicily, where he had gone alone attended only by a servant, Gennaro, who had been in the service of English families before, and against the advice of his friends, having parted company with the Froudes who went back to England. 'I hope it is not presumptuous,' he wrote to his friend H. W. Wilberforce on August 4, 1833, 'but from the beginning of my illness I had so strong a feeling on my mind that I should recover, that, whatever I did in the way of preparation for death . . . was done as a mere matter of duty . . . I had once, doubtless when I felt myself lonely, quite a revelation come upon me of God's love to His elect, and felt as if I were one . . . not that I can describe the feeling in words. Then I was much relieved next day, by being able to discover, as I thought, sins in my conduct which had led God to fight against me. . . . Now I came to think that there was something of wilfulness in my coming to Sicily. . . . And then I felt more than I had done the wilfulness of my character generally. . . . And then I recollected that the very day before I left Oxford, I had preached a Sermon against Wilfulness, so that I seemed to be predicting my own condemnation. And I went on to ask myself whether I had not cherished resentment against the Provost.'

In the Sermon against Wilfulness just mentioned Newman had said that 'the pliant and amiable by nature, generally speaking, are not the subjects of great purposes. . . . But those minds, which naturally most resemble the aboriginal chaos, contain within them the elements of a marvellous creation of light and beauty, if they but open their hearts to the effectual power of the Holy Spirit. Pride and sullenness, obstinacy and impetuosity, then become transformed into the zeal, firmness, and high-mindedness of religious Faith.'

Here Newman unwittingly drew a portrait of himself; for he, too, for all his attractiveness, was by no means 'pliant and amiable by nature', as he had shown in the tutorship controversy, when he wrote of himself that 'when he had a clear view of a matter, [he] was accustomed to formulate it, and was apt to be . . . considered irreverent and rude in the nakedness of his analysis, and un-measured and even impatient in enforcing it'.

When a year later, in August 1834, Newman drew up an account of his illness to clarify his own mind, he was even more deeply convinced about its providential aspect. 'I could almost think the devil saw I am to be a means of usefulness, and tried to destroy me. The fever was most dangerous . . . yet all through I had a confident feeling *I should recover*. I told my Servant so, and gave as a reason . . . that "I thought God had some work for me".' So his interpretation of his Sicilian ordeal had changed. He no longer saw it as a divine punishment for his sins but as the devil's efforts to destroy him, because he was going to do work for God. It is significant of Newman that he took little notice of the natural causes of his illness—after all, a typhoid epidemic was raging in Sicily at the time, as he himself mentioned in a letter to his friend Rogers of June 5, 1833, though he thought it was scarlet fever, and so it was quite natural that he should have caught it, ex-hausted by insufficient food and sleep as he was at the time. But as the invisible world was more real to him than the visible, he saw the natural causes as no more than the visible instruments of invisible powers and himself as the object of their love or hatred. In his first spiritual experience at the age of fifteen he had the vivid impression that he was elected to eternal glory; now he was convinced that 'God had some work' for him in England. But this conviction was accompanied by a searching insight into

himself, which he described in his memoir of 1834 and which is so
important that it must be quoted extensively:

'. . . the self-reproaching feelings increased. I seemed to see
more and more my utter hollowness. I began to think of all my
professed principles, and felt they were mere intellectual deduc-
tions from one or two admitted truths. I compared myself with
Keble, and felt that I was merely developing his, not my convictions. I know I had very *clear* thoughts about this then, and, I
believe in the main true ones. Indeed this is how I look on myself:
very much (as the illustration goes) as a pane of glass, which
transmits heat being cold itself. I have a vivid perception of the
consequences of certain admitted principles, have a considerable
intellectual capacity of drawing them out, have the refinement to
admire them, and a rhetorical or histrionic power to represent
them; and, having no great (i.e. no vivid) love of this world,
whether riches, honours, or anything else, and some firmness and
natural dignity of character, take the profession of them upon me,
as I might sing a tune which I liked—loving the Truth, but not
possessing it—for I believe myself at heart to be hollow—i.e. with
little love, little self denial. I believe I have some faith, that is all
—and as to my sins, they need my possessing no little amount of
faith to set against them and gain their remission. By the bye, this
statement will account for it how I can preach the Truth without
thinking much of myself. Arnold in his letter to Grant about me,
accuses me among others of identifying high excellence with
certain peculiarities of my own—i.e. preaching myself. . . . Still
more serious thoughts came over me. I though I had been very
self willed about the Tutorship affair—and now I viewed my
whole course as one of presumption. . . . Then I bitterly blamed
myself, as disrespectful and insulting to the Provost, my superior.
So keenly did I feel this, that I dictated to myself (as it were) a
letter which I was to send . . . on my getting back to England,
stating in strong terms my self reproach; and I was not to preach
at St Mary's or anywhere for a length of time as a penitent unworthy to show himself. . . . Yet still I said to myself "I have not
sinned against light".'

In the strange clarity when, as he wrote, 'all my feelings, painful and pleasant, were heightened by somewhat of delirium', Newman took stock of himself. He realized that he had certain natural advantages, especially no great love of the world and its prizes such as riches and honours, so much coveted by most men. Further, he had a strong character which made it comparatively easy for him to govern his lower instincts. But as all these were natural advantages, he felt that he had no right to attribute them to his own efforts. Nor did his preaching, as he thought, have its roots in the depths of his own being, but rather in his intellect, which drew consequences from certain principles which his 'rhetorical power' then impressed on his hearers. He seemed to himself like a pane of glass that remains cold while transmitting heat.

Were these only the exaggerated imaginings of a feverish brain or, as Newman himself evidently believed, his real faults? That there was more than a grain of truth in them can hardly be denied. The man who had lain on his sofa 'writhing' because he thought he had made a fool of himself at his first University sermon and who, as we shall see, could impress on a dying man his sinfulness and corruption was not yet a saint. If he had no desire for honours, he was not prepared to endure scorn, and Thomas Arnold (of Rugby) was certainly not altogether wrong in saying that Newman was in a certain way preaching himself. For he preached against faults such as the danger of intellectual accomplishments and ambitious thoughts, which were peculiarly his own, and he insisted upon the reality of the unseen world, which was so familiar to him.

But when he accused himself of 'loving the Truth, but not possessing it', of having little love and little self-denial he did less than justice to himself. For every preacher must set before his hearers the high ideals of the Christian life, and the more sincere he is, the greater self-knowledge he has, the more will he be conscious of ever falling far behind the virtues he preaches. Newman had been given positions of great responsibility when he was still very young; he had preached often with great severity; it was not surprising that at a testing time such as the weeks in Sicily he should have realized that the sanctity he had preached had not yet been reached in his own life, that there was a gap between the words of the preacher and the deeds of the man. Yet again and again the conviction asserted itself that he had 'not sinned against light'.

It is not easy to determine what he meant by this. He was evidently aware that whatever his conscience accused him of, he had not lost God's friendship. His sins had been sins of human weakness, but he had never deliberately done what he knew to be wrong.

But what of the 'utter hollowness' of which he had become conscious? For a man so deeply aware of the invisible world and of his own duties, so full of original ideas and profound thought to accuse himself of hollowness certainly sounds unreal, not to say hypocritical. But Newman was never given to unreal pronouncements, let alone hypocritical ones. During these decisive days in Sicily he had come face to face with himself and with God's demands on him, he had quite evidently had a very strong intuition of his own vocation. Ever since Isaiah's cry: 'Woe is me! For I am lost; for I am a man of unclean lips' man's response to a divine call has been the acknowledgement of his own unworthiness. Newman's awareness of his 'utter hollowness' was but the response to his intuition of having God's work to do in England, to a 'strange feeling' he had had when setting out on his journey to Sicily, where he fell ill, 'that God meets those who go on in *His way,* who remember Him in His way, in the paths of the Lord, that I must put myself in His path'. For him this illness and its strange accompaniments of spiritual lucidity were a meeting with God, and the insight he received into his own self was a divine illumination, showing him his faults, especially his wilfulness, and the difference there still was between word and deed.

The outcome of this purification by illness and intuitive self-knowledge was a peace and surrender to God's will that found expression in one of his finest and best-known poems:

Lead, Kindly Light, amid the encircling gloom
    Lead Thou me on!
The night is dark, and I am far from home—
    Lead Thou me on!
Keep Thou my feet; I do not ask to see
The distant scene—one step enough for me.

I was not ever thus, nor pray'd that Thou
    Shouldst lead me on.
I loved to choose and see my path, but now
    Lead Thou me on.
I loved the garish day, and, spite of fears,
Pride ruled my will: remember not past years.

So long Thy power hath blest me, sure it still
    Will lead me on,
O'er moor and fen, o'er crag and torrent, till
    The night is gone;
And with the morn those angel faces smile
Which I have loved long since, and lost awhile.

All the spirituality of the maturing Newman is in these lines. From his youth he had had the strong conviction of being divinely guided; but he felt that he had made his own plans rather than let himself be led by Providence, and now, after his experience in Sicily, he recognized this as pride. He will make no more plans but only follow where the kindly divine light guides him through the night of this life, until the powers of the invisible world he has loved for so long, the 'angel faces', will smile at him.

Exactly a year later he could write: 'Now it certainly is remarkable that a new and large sphere of action has opened upon me from the very moment I returned . . . and altogether my name, which was not known out of Oxford circles before I went abroad, is now known pretty generally. My Sermons have sold very well. Now in all this there seems something remarkable and providential. O my God, keep me still from being the sport and victim of Satan. By Thy Mercies in Thy Son's Holy Table which I have this day partaken, be to me a Saviour.'

For by now the Oxford Movement, whose leading mind Newman was, had begun to imbue the Church of England with a new spirituality.

3 THE SPIRITUALITY OF
THE OXFORD MOVEMENT

In his *Apologia* Newman himself assigned the beginning of the Oxford Movement to Keble's sermon on 'National Apostasy', preached in the University Pulpit on July 14, 1833, and he has been followed in this attribution by many later writers. But in his book on Newman, Dr F. L. Cross has called this a 'myth', and proved convincingly that the sermon made very little impression at the time, except on Newman himself who immediately asked for some copies of it. For he had returned from Italy just a few days before he heard it, full of new vigour and the conviction that the Church of England was in a bad state and something must be done about it. Keble expressed exactly what Newman and also the other leaders of the Movement felt, hence he dated the beginning of the Movement from this sermon. He felt that a new spirit must be instilled into the Church of England, a spirit that was to be primarily a spirit of penance, because sin was taken so very lightly in the contemporary Establishment. For this reason, as we shall see, the spirituality Newman preached was extremely severe; it has sometimes been called Calvinistic or Jansenistic, and it certainly has features resembling these systems; but, on the other hand, the early Church, too, had been very strict in its treatment of sinners, and in a Church like the Church of England of the time, which had no practice of individual confession and absolution and no practical moral theology determining the seriousness of the various sins, an individual clergyman had no authoritative standards to go by. And because the majority of the clergy were inclined to take neither doctrine nor sin very seriously, Newman initiated a

47

movement that was to insist on both, sound doctrine and individual sanctity.

'The Times are very Evil'

But what was to be done to instil this new spirit into the Church of England? Newman was fundamentally a man of letters rather than a man of action, and so he conceived the idea of publishing tracts to deal with the most important subjects that were in his mind.

The first of them appeared in September 1833. It begins, characteristically, with a personal remark and goes on in the tone of the Old Testament prophets. 'I am but one of yourselves,' he writes, 'a Presbyter [using the Biblical word for priest]; and therefore I conceal my name, lest I should take too much on myself by speaking in my own person. Yet speak I must; for the times are very evil, yet no one speaks against them.'

The times are very evil—this had already been one of his leitmotifs as a preacher before his experience in Sicily, and it continued to dominate his later sermons as well. As early as 1825 he had told his congregation that 'one of those sins which belongs to our age more than to another, is desire of a greater portion of worldly goods than God has given us—ambitiousness and covetousness in one shape or another'. And in 1829, the year of Catholic emancipation, he had thundered from the pulpit of St Mary's—though 'thunder' is perhaps not quite the right word, because he spoke always rather quietly: 'Now, as to the temper of this country, consider fairly, is there any place, any persons, any work, which our countrymen will not connect themselves with, in the way of trade or business? For the sake of gain, do we not put aside all considerations of principle as unseasonable and almost absurd? . . . Do we care what side of a quarrel, civil, political, or international, we take, so that we gain by it? Do we not serve in war, do we not become debaters and advocates, do we not form associations and parties, with the supreme object of preserving property, or making it? Do we not support religion for the sake of peace and good order? Do we not measure its importance by its efficacy in securing these objects? . . . Should we not easily resign ourselves to its overthrow, could it be proved to us that it endangered the State, involved the prospect of civil disturbances or embarrassed the Government?' Seven years later, in a sermon on 'The Incarnate Son', he again deplored 'the eagerness of the great mass of men . . . after gain, after national aggrandizement, after speculations which promise public or private advantage'. No foreign critic could have been harder on the England of the early days of the industrial revolution than this unworldly Fellow of Oriel at whose sight, as a contemporary has described it, 'light-hearted undergraduates would drop their voices and whisper, "There's Newman!" when, head thrust forward and gaze fixed as though on some vision seen only by himself, with swift, noiseless step, he glided by'.

A Superficial Christianity

For Newman the tremendous success of the expanding British Empire was nothing admirable; on the contrary, he saw it as the greatest danger to genuine Christianity. For the national religion was most intimately bound up with this empire and its government, which encroached more and more on the rights of the Church 'as by law established'. He described this religion in two sermons, both preached in 1832, one in the *Parochial and Plain Sermons*, on 'The Religion of the Day', the other his University Sermon on 'Wilfulness, the Sin of Saul', delivered immediately before his departure for Italy. Both sermons show how much the state of the Church of England had been in his thoughts at that time, confirming the view of Dr Cross that it did not need Keble's sermon on National Apostasy to impress this subject on his mind.

In the sermon on 'The Religion of the Day' Newman complains that this religion stresses only 'the brighter side of the Gospel—its tidings of comfort, its precepts of love; all darker, deeper views of man's condition and prospects being comparatively forgotten. . . . Everything is bright and cheerful. Religion is pleasant and

D

easy; benevolence is the chief virtue; intolerance, bigotry, excess of zeal, are the first of sins. Austerity is an absurdity.' And in the University Sermon he castigated 'the irreverence towards Antiquity, the unscrupulous and wanton violation of the commands and usages of our forefathers, the undoing of their benefactions, the profanation of the Church . . . the growing indifference to the Catholic Creed, the sceptical objections to portions of its doctrine, the arguings and discussings and comparings and correctings and rejectings, and all the train of presumptuous exercises, to which its sacred articles are subjected'.

The Movement of the Tracts was to counteract these evils. What was to be the remedy? It was, to put it in a nutshell, a return to the sources, to the sources of the Christian Church in general (that is to say to Scripture and the early Fathers), and of the Church of England in particular, the great Anglican divines of the sixteenth and seventeenth centuries such as Hooker, Hammond and Bishop Ken. For Newman had now come to reject Protestantism as well as Roman Catholicism; he sought a middle way between the two, the famous *Via Media*, which, he believed, was the true Christianity, equally removed from the diminishments of Lutherans and Calvinists and the accretions of late medieval and Tridentine religion, while retaining intact its Biblical basis.

In *Tract 3*, which opposed suggested changes in the liturgy of the Prayer Book, Newman rejected the idea of leaving out the so called imprecatory Psalms.* 'If this were to happen,' he writes, 'we certainly countenance the notion of the day, that love and love only is in the Gospel the character of Almighty God and the duty of regenerate man; whereas the Gospel, rightly understood, shows His Infinite Holiness and Justice as well as His Infinite Love; and it enjoins on men the duties of zeal towards Him, hatred of sin, and separation from sinners, as well as that of kindness and charity.' In his stress on the infinite holiness of God Newman went so far as very nearly to obliterate the humanity of Christ. He had himself experienced the attraction of contemporary religious

---

* Those Psalms which ask for divine vengeance, e.g. Pss. 58; 69:23-9; 109:5-19 and others.

liberalism and therefore attacked it all the more vigorously, as he himself admits in *Tract 73* 'On the Introduction of Rationalistic Principles into Religion'. There he writes: 'The books of the day are so full of its [liberalism's] evil doctrine in a modified shape, if not in its grosser forms, the principles of the nation are so instinct with it or based in it, that the best perhaps that can be said of any of us, or at most of all but a few, is, that they have escaped from it, "so as by fire", and that the loudness of their warning is but a consequence of past danger, terror, and flight.'

Newman's Christ *dehumanized*

Newman's warnings were certainly very loud, indeed, and he did not always escape the danger of falling into the opposite extremes, a fundamentalism that took all Scripture literally, a view of Christ that almost obliterated his humanity and a severe morality that would make practically no allowance for human weakness. In the same *Tract 73* he criticized a contemporary author who had written of Christ that he 'had a taste for beauty, both of nature and art'. Newman comments: 'Let us think seriously, is Christ God, or is He not? if so, can we dare talk of Him as having "a taste for nature"? . . . we have utterly no warrant to speak, of the Person of the Eternal Word as thinking and feeling like a mere man, like a child, or a boy, as simply ignorant, imperfect, and dependent on the creature. . . .' But Scripture itself speaks of him as truly human; he was certainly dependent on his Mother to be born and nurtured, on both Mary and Joseph to be taken to Egypt, and he expressed very human anguish in the garden of Gethsemane, to take only a few examples. And when the unfortunate author under criticism dares to write that the courage of Jesus when meeting Judas and the soldiers far exceeds that of Napoleon, Newman is so horrified that he feels he has incurred 'some ceremonial pollution by repeating such miserable words'.

In his reaction against the purely human Christ of rationalism he often preaches a Christ whose divinity is emphasized to such a degree as to make him almost unapproachable. Even when washing Peter's feet: 'see,' Newman writes, 'if it were not calculated (assuredly it was) to humble, to awe, and subdue the very person to whom He ministered. When He taught, warned, pitied, prayed for, His ignorant hearers, He never allowed them to relax their reverence or to overlook His condescension. . . . He who was so reserved in His communications of Himself, even when He came to minister, much more would withdraw Himself from the eyes of men when He was exalted over all things.' In a sermon on St Stephen he tells us that by seeing how far Christ's true servants surpass ourselves, 'we learn to shrink before His ineffable purity'; and in one on 'Christ, the Son of God made Man', he emphasizes that, 'He was not man in exactly the same sense in which any one of us is a man. . . . We may not speak of Him as we speak of any individual man, acting from and governed by a human intelligence within Him' and 'When He wept at the grave of Lazarus . . . or had compassion on the multitudes, He manifested the tender mercy, the compassion . . . of Almighty God . . . through the outlets of that manhood with which He had clothed Himself'.

Newman's unapproachable Christ could seem almost the Christ of Jansenism. But we must remember that Newman's preaching was directed against both the sentimentalized Jesus of the evangelicals and the denial of his divinity by the 'liberals'. For this reason he emphasized the divine authority of Christ, and pictured him as the Lord rather than as the brotherly high priest of the Epistle to the Hebrews, who was 'not a high priest who is unable to sympathize with our weaknesses, but one who in every respect has been tempted as we are, yet without sinning'. Newman's Christ demanded above all reverence, and reverence was one of the main themes of the leader of the early Oxford Movement.

In 1838 he preached a sermon on the subject, reiterating what he had said in the tract that men were 'apt to use rude, familiar, profane language, concerning their God's childhood, and youth, and ministry, though He is their God.' He even objects to the Lord's name being used in prayer; because the translators of the

Old Testament refrained from using the sacred name of God, 'substituting the word "Lord" out of reverence. Now,' he continues, 'the persons in question delight in a familiar use, in prayers and hymns and conversation, of that Name by which they designate Him before whom the Angels tremble. Not even our fellowmen do we freely call by their own names, unless we are at our ease with them; yet sinners can bear to be familiar with the Name by which they know the Most High has distinguished Himself from all creatures. If a man believes Him present, he will shrink from addressing Him familiarly. . . .'

Yet Our Lord himself taught us to address God as 'Our Father', surely a most familiar term of address; and he told his disciples that he no longer called them servants, but friends, while St Paul taught his converts that they were members of the body of Christ, a most intimate relationship. But Newman was still so steeped in the Old Testament—just under a third of his *Parochial and Plain Sermons* were preached on Old Testament texts, and in the others, too, the Old Testament is quoted constantly—that he was often inclined to use its language of awe rather than the New Testament language of love. In another sermon, entitled 'Reverence in Worship', he developed the same theme. He considered it irreverent to judge the sermon and even to pray in one's own words when in church, because that would be doing things in one's own way whereas, he asserts, the apostles 'never spoke their own words in solemn worship', and in another sermon he even went so far as to say that 'common men have no right to use prayers which advanced Christians use without offending', when it must be asked who is to decide whether anyone is sufficiently advanced to use which prayers.

A Pessimistic View of the World

This insistence on the distance between God and men which allows of no familiar approach is intimately connected with a moral pessimism which Newman shares with the other leaders of the Oxford Movement, and which comes out particularly in his

sermons of this period. 'This world is Satan's efficacious Form, it
is the instrument through which he spreads out in order and
attractiveness his many snares,' he writes in a sermon on prayer.
As we have seen before, he regarded the beauties of the world
as temptations rather than as ways leading to the Creator, considering it an insult to Christ that he should have had 'a taste
for beauty'. For 'the world in which our duties lie, is as waste as
the wilderness', it is a 'wretched deceiving world'; life itself 'is
scarcely more than an accident of our being . . . only intended
to answer the purpose of trying whether we will serve God or no',
and he headed one of his sermons 'Scripture a record of human
sorrow', in which he said that God himself had given us a 'dark
view of the world'. Considering how much both the Old and the
New Testament say about joy and rejoicing it is rather difficult to
agree with this statement. In those days Newman also rejected as
sinful or leading to sin activities and aspirations not generally
regarded as such by Christian theologians. His views on the subject are expressed most forcefully in a sermon preached in 1831 on
the feast of St Luke and entitled 'The Danger of Accomplishments'. Now Newman was himself a highly educated and 'accomplished' person, therefore he does not, of course, reject intellectual
and other accomplishments as such. But he points out the possibilities of their abuse with a vigour and insistence surprising in a
university don.

He sees the danger of what he calls 'an elegant and polite
education' in that 'it teaches to think, speak, and be affected aright,
without forcing us to practise what is right'. He gives the reading
of novels as an example of what he means. 'Such works,' he
admits, 'contain many good sentiments (I am taking the better
sort of them): characters too are introduced, virtuous, noble,
patient under suffering, and triumphing at length over misfortune.
The great truths of religion are upheld, we will suppose, and
enforced; and our affections excited and interested in what is good
and true. But it is all fiction; it does not exist out of a book which
contains the beginning and end of it. We have nothing *to do*; we
read, are affected, softened or roused, and that is all. . . . Now

observe the effect of this. God has made us feel in order that we may *go on to act* in consequence of feeling; if then we allow our feelings to be excited without acting upon them, we do mischief to the moral system within us. . . .' For, according to Newman, feelings and intellectual or spiritual enjoyment that do not result in moral action are not only useless but actually harmful. He exempts from this statement not even religious art, because he considers that it leads to cultivating religious sentiments rather than religious practice. Neither religious poetry nor even the chant of the Psalms finds favour with the young preacher; in fact 'these are especially likely to make us unmanly, if we are not on our guard, as exciting emotions without insuring correspondent practice . . . for here I mean by unmanliness the inability to do with ourselves what we wish—the saying fine things and yet lying slothfully on our couch'.

What he abhors particularly is that in the religious literature of his time a false impression is given of the Christian life: 'Pictures are drawn of *complete* virtue; little is said about failures, and little or nothing of the drudgery of ordinary, every-day obedience, which is neither poetical nor interesting.'

The sermon ends with practical advice on how to treat such dangerous 'lighter occupations' as novel reading, music and the like. First, we must not give too much time to them, 'and next, we must never allow ourselves to read works of fiction or poetry, or to interest ourselves in the fine arts for the mere sake of the things themselves: but keep in mind all along that we are Christians and accountable beings, who have fixed principles of right and wrong, by which all things must be tried, and have religious habits to be matured within them, towards which all things are to be made subservient.'

This sermon shows with particular clarity how deeply rooted were the evangelical principles Newman had imbibed in his youth. He does not forbid novel or poetry reading altogether, but it must not be enjoyed for its own sake. Nor are spiritual books or spiritual conversations of any value unless they lead directly to moral action; in fact they are, on the whole, dangerous rather than useful. This extremely negative attitude to all that makes life as well as religion attractive to the senses may perhaps also be explained as a reaction against certain temptations Newman felt in himself. As we have seen, and as also emerges quite clearly from his autobiographical writings of this period, he was especially afraid that his intellectual activities might harm his relation with God, and his great love of music and poetry may have been a temptation to indulge overmuch in religious feelings.

Some of his letters and notes written during these early years show the same severe—at times it might almost be called priggish —attitude. He spoke for example to an old coachman on his deathbed, who felt that the load of sin had been taken away from him, 'very strongly on our being sinful and corrupt till death, on the necessity of sin being found a burden *always*, on the fear of self-deception', and he deliberately made 'holiness', not 'comfort' the end of his preaching and ministry. Hence Christian endeavour itself is seen through very dark glasses. In one of his early University Sermons Newman affirms that 'it is by no means clear that Christianity has at any time been of any great spiritual advantage to the world at large . . . it has ever been a restraint on the world rather than a guide to personal virtue and perfection on a large scale; its fruits are negative.' Now it is quite true, of course, that the heights of Christian perfection have always been scaled only by the few; but it can hardly be doubted that Christianity has had a very beneficial influence in the past, for example in the civilization of the Germanic tribes in the so-called Dark Ages, and that it has taught the world moral principles that have influenced even non-Christian civilizations.

Sin

Newman's early pessimism affected not only his view of Christianity at large but also that of individual Christians. One of the most disheartening of his ideas is that temptation necessarily involves sin, that even if we involuntarily, by a mere passing feeling, respond to things like 'the world's praise, power, ease, indulgence' we have already sinned. Thus it is not surprising that Newman should tell his congregation: 'Be sure that the longer you live, and the holier you become, you will only perceive that misery more clearly. The less of it you have, the more it will oppress you; its full draught does but confuse and stupefy you; as you come to yourself, your misery begins.'

Such has not been the experience of the saints. Though many of them frequently accused themselves of their sinfulness which they saw in the light of the perfect purity of God, they were never oppressed, let alone 'stupefied' by it, for they knew that God's grace was ever more powerful than their imperfections. Newman frequently insists on 'the difficulty of attaining Heaven', and he states that even 'the better sort of Christians . . . are deformed in stature, they are not upright, they do not walk perfectly with God. And you cannot tell why it is;—they have ever lived religiously—they have been removed from temptation, had good training and instruction, and they fulfil their calling, are good husbands or wives, good parents, good neighbours—still when you come to know them well, there is in them this or that great inconsistency.' Newman traces this to some 'fault out of sight', giving as an example 'the indulgence of harsh, unforgiving thoughts' for a few minutes each day or each week. 'Who can tell but a soul so circumstanced,' he continues, 'may be severed from the grace of the Ordinances [i.e. sacraments], though he partakes them outwardly, and is but existing upon and exhausting the small treasure of strength and life which is laid up within him? . . . such sin shuts us out from God's presence, and obstructs the channels by which He gives us grace.'

These are very harsh words indeed. Surely, if a man is an exemplary Christian in every other way, the grace of the sacraments should be strong enough to overcome this one 'fault out of sight?' But Newman goes even further than this. In his opinion even infants can commit sins that will have evil effects throughout their life; for, he argues, 'as sicknesses and accidents then [in infancy] happening permanently affect their body, though they recollect nothing of them, there is no extravagance in the idea that passing

sins then contracted and forgotten for ever afterwards, should so
affect the soul as to cause those moral differences between man and
man which . . . are too clear to be denied. And with this fearful
thought before us of the responsibility attaching to the first years
of our life, how miserable is it to reflect on the other hand that
children are commonly treated as if they were not responsible. . . .'
But sin can only exist in morally responsible people; surely a
naughty three-year-old cannot be said to 'sin' in the proper sense
of the word, because sins are a deliberate offence against God,
and infants are unable to commit them. It is, of course true, as
Newman continues in the same sermon on 'The Moral Consequences of Single Sins' that bad example and other educational
defects will have far-reaching consequences in adult life; but these
can then not be attributed to the infant but to the adults entrusted
with its upbringing; Christ himself placed the responsibility on the
adult, not on the child when he said: 'Whoever causes one of
these little ones who believe in me to sin, it would be better for
him to have a great millstone fastened round his neck and to be
drowned in the depth of the sea' (Matthew 18:6). The sin is the
sin of the adult, not the sin of the child.

It is only consistent that in Newman's view the effects of sin
can never be wholly obliterated, even after conversion, and he was
influenced by the penitential practice of the early Church when he
exacted a long and severe testing period before sinners could hope
to enjoy a fully Christian life again. In one of his sermons he
addressed his hearers in the following frightening terms: 'Till
you know the weight of your sins, and not in mere imagination,
but in practice, not so as merely to confess it in a formal phrase
of lamentation, but daily and in your heart in secret, you cannot
embrace the offer of mercy held out to you in the Gospel. . . .
How long and earnestly must you pray, how many years must
you pass in careful obedience, before you have any right to lay
aside sorrow, and to rejoice in the Lord?' Indeed, Newman considered a previously immoral life 'a grievous permanent hindrance
and curse to a man after he has turned to God'; he has not told
us how he could reconcile this with Christ's own words that there

is more joy in heaven over one sinner who repents than over ninety-nine just men.

He further alleges that no penitent has ever been 'honoured with any important station in the [early] Church'—a statement which certainly does not correspond to the facts. We need only think of the greatest doctor of the Latin Church, St Augustine, who became an extremely influential bishop fairly soon after being converted from an immoral life. Newman overlooked this, for he was of the opinion 'that the indulgence of early passions, though forgotten now, and the misapplication of reason in our youth, have left an indelibly evil character upon our heart'. It is significant, too, that in an essay on the conversion of St Augustine he left out completely the Saint's difficulties in breaking away from his mistress; indeed she and Augustine's son are not so much as mentioned, and the only habit Newman singles out as having been given up by St Augustine is 'profane swearing'! At that time Newman did not subscribe to the principle that one should hate the sin, but love the sinner, for in a sermon significantly entitled 'Jewish Zeal, a Pattern to Christians', he writes: 'We hate sinners, by putting them out of our sight, as if they were not, by annihilating them, in our affection.' This from a minister of him who was accused of consorting with sinners and publicans is strange, to say the least. But then Newman considers that the Church is not a Church of sinners as well as of saints, for he writes in *The State of Salvation* that 'the Christian state does not shelter a man who sins, but it lets him drop', for, he says, 'the Gospel only knows of justified saints; if a saint sins, he ceases to be justified, and becomes a *condemned* sinner'. Newman's harshness to sinners was certainly a reaction against what he called 'the religion of the day' that thought of the Gospel exclusively as a message of love and joy, leaving out completely its reverse side, the threats of punishment and the doctrine of hell. Newman went to the other extreme, emphasizing the dark side to such an extent as to take away the joy and the glory; he preaches, as it were, a perpetual Lent.

Fear of Emotions

One of the most characteristic expressions of this attitude is his sermon preached on Easter Day 1838—that feast when the Churches of both Eastern and Western Christendom break out into veritable paeans of joy, when all the candles burn, the bells peal, and the Alleluias ring out, because the long fast of Lent and the intense sorrowing of Holy Week are ended, Christ is risen indeed and Christians are bidden to rejoice, in church as well as at home in their Lord's victory over death. Not so Newman. He tells his hearers that 'they are disposed rather to muse and be at peace, than to use many words; for their joy has been so much a child of sorrow, is of so transmuted and complex a nature . . . that though it is a joy only the greater from the contrast, it is not, cannot be, as if it had never been sorrow . . . for in this does Christian mirth differ from worldly, that it is subdued; and how shall it be subdued except that the past keeps its hold upon us, and while it warns and sobers us, actually indisposes and tames our flesh against indulgence? . . . Our Festivals are preceded by humiliation, that we may keep them duly; not boisterously or fanatically, but in a refined, subdued chastised spirit, which is the true rejoicing in the Lord.'

The Invisible World

Newman was once accused of only preaching himself; there is more than a grain of truth in this. Though he could be passionate in his denunciation of sin and his insistence on following the commandments, the spirituality he recommended at this time was curiously staid and unemotional. The Catholic Church's compassion for sinners and its ability to satisfy the whole human being, his need of joy as well as of penance, were as yet foreign to him. Moreover, he lived to an extraordinary degree in what he calls 'the unseen world'; this was his spiritual home, therefore he could not always understand the needs of ordinary men and women, to whom this world was unfamiliar. He himself wrote in a letter to a friend that he wished he lived as much in the unseen world as he thought he did not live in this—this was the cause of his great spiritual strength and his influence on others but also of his lack of social sense. For to him, as he wrote in the first volume of the *Via Media*, 'Christianity is a supernatural gift, originating and living in the unseen world and only extending into this.' Therefore the invisible is the only true reality, for 'that which is seen is not real', because it is material and transitory. Christians, therefore, are already here on earth 'in Heaven, in the world of spirits, and are placed in the way of all manner of invisible influences'.

He developed his thought about it in a sermon on 2 Corinthians 4:18, 'While we look not at the things which are seen, but at the things which are not seen', preached in 1837 and called 'The Invisible World'. 'In spite of this universal world which we see,' he writes, 'there is another world, quite as far-spreading, quite as close to us, and more wonderful; another world all around us, though we see it not, and more wonderful than the world we see, for this reason if for no other, that we do not see it.' 'We are then in a world of spirits, as well as in a world of sense, and we hold communion with it, and take part in it, though we are not conscious of doing so.'

This reality of the 'unseen world' Newman tries to impress on his hearers again and again; for it is not only the true reality underlying and surrounding this visible world, the awareness of it is also the most effective bulwark against the materialism of the time. For the only legitimate use of this world, as he still affirmed in a sermon on 'Unreal Words' preached in 1839 is 'to make us seek for another. It does its part when it repels us and disgusts us and drives us elsewhere', and in 1840 he even told his congregation that 'This world is a dream—you will get no good from it'. When he speaks about the Church he does not stress the outward ceremonial, though this, too, is necessary, but he insists that the visible Church leads to the invisible world. 'The ordinances we behold,' he says in a sermon on 'The Visible Church', 'force the unseen truth upon our senses. The very dis-

position of the building, the subdued light, the aisles, the Altar
. . . are figures of things unseen, and stimulate our fainting faith.
We seem to see the heavenly courts. . . . Even to those, I say,
who live to the world, the mere Sunday attendance at Church is
a continual memento on their conscience, giving them a glimpse
of things unseen, and rescuing them in a measure from the servi-
tude of Mammon or of Belial.' The sacraments no less than private
prayer introduce the Christian into this invisible world, and when
we do battle for the Lord we are assisted by its powers. For the
blessings Christians enjoy are unseen, and for this very reason they
are higher than the visible ones of the Chosen People in the Old
Covenant. 'All Christians,' therefore, 'are kings in God's sight;
they are kings in His unseen kingdom. . . . They seem like other
men, but they have crowns on their heads, and glorious robes
around them, and Angels to wait on them, though our bodily
eyes see it not.'

This world of the angels was so real to him that he discovered
its activity even behind the world of nature, a view in which he
was confirmed by the Greek Fathers, especially by Origen. So he
wrote in his sermon on 'The Powers of Nature': 'the sin of what
is called an educated age, such as our own, is . . . to account
slightly of them [the angels], or not at all; to ascribe all we see
around us not to their agency, but to certain assumed laws of
nature . . . this is the danger of many (so-called) philosophical
pursuits . . . chemistry, geology, and the like, the danger, that
is, of resting in things seen, and forgetting unseen things, and our
ignorance about them. . . . How do the wind and water, earth
and fire, move? Now here Scripture interposes, and seems to tell
us, that all this wonderful harmony is the work of Angels. Those
events which we ascribe to chance as the weather, or to nature
as the seasons, are duties done to that God who maketh His Angels
to be winds and His Ministers a flame of fire. . . . Thus, whenever we look abroad, we are reminded of those most gracious and
holy Beings, the servants of the Holiest, who deign to minister
to the heirs of salvation. Every breath of air and ray of light and
heat, every beautiful prospect, is, as it were, the skirts of their

mysticism

garments, the waving of the robes of those whose faces see God in heaven. And I put it to any one, whether it is not as philosophical and as full of intellectual enjoyment, to refer the movements of the natural world to them, as to attempt to explain them by certain theories of science.'

Here speaks Newman the student of the Fathers as well as Newman the poet and the lover of the Bible, who felt so deeply the need to lead men back to familiarity with the unseen world. For this emphasis on the ministry of the angels in nature, which is quite foreign to us and which a thinker like Teilhard de Chardin would have vigorously rejected, was also caused by Newman's fear that the scientific progress of mankind that was just beginning to accelerate in his time would estrange man completely from God and from divine things. He did not despise science—indeed, he was himself a very good mathematician—but he wanted it to remain subservient to God and to the invisible world. For him nature was still animated by unseen powers and was therefore to be treated with reverence, whereas if a man were to hold 'that the Order of Nature, which he partially discerns, will stand in the place of the God who made it, and that all things continue and move on, not by His will and power, and the agency of the thousands and ten thousands of His unseen Servants, but by fixed laws, self-caused and self-sustained, what a poor weak worm and miserable sinner he becomes!'

typically Victorian

It should be noted, however, that although Newman retained his keen perception of the unseen world throughout his life, he later abandoned the idea of the angelic office in nature. For such an opinion is not only impossible to hold in view of modern scientific developments, it is also in no way bound up with Christian philosophy; St Thomas Aquinas, for example, gives its right ful place to natural causation without postulating angelic activity in this sphere.

Sacraments and the Indwelling of the Spirit

How is a man going to be admitted to this unseen world?

Since the Church is, as it were, the steward of the mysteries of this world, the gate through which he must invariably pass is baptism; for, writes Newman, in his sermon on 'The World's Benefactors', 'when we are made Christians, we are baptized "into that within the veil", we are brought near to an innumerable company of angels . . . and surely we ought to cultivate the habitual feeling, that they see us in our most private deeds, and most carefully guarded solitudes.'

Newman elaborates this theme in a later sermon on 'The Gift of the Spirit', preached in 1835, in which he speaks about illumination, a term frequently used by the Fathers as a synonym for baptism. This illumination he calls 'the heavenly gift . . . that unspeakable Gospel privilege, which is an earnest and portion of heavenly glory, of the holiness and blessedness of Angels—a present entrance into the next world, opened upon our souls through participation of the Word Incarnate, ministered to us by the Holy Ghost. Such is the mysterious state in which Christians stand. . . . They are in Heaven, in the world of spirits, and are placed in the way of all manner of invisible influences.' These influences may be summed up in the indwelling of the Holy Spirit. This doctrine was quite prominent in the spirituality of the Greek Fathers as well as in the teaching and experience of the mystics, though it was somewhat neglected in the arid theology of the nineteenth century.

Newman stressed the working of the Spirit in the Christian in the very beginning of his preaching career. In his sermon on 'Holiness Necessary for Future Blessedness', preached in 1826, after exhorting his congregation to be 'content with nothing short of perfection', he assures them of the divine help in the difficult task of achieving holiness: 'While we thus labour to mould our hearts after the pattern of the holiness of our Heavenly Father,' he says, 'it is our comfort to know . . . that we are not left to ourselves, but that the Holy Ghost is graciously present with us, and enables us to triumph over, and to change our own minds. It is a comfort and encouragement, while it is an anxious and awful thing, to know that God works in and through us. We are the instruments, but we are only the instruments, of our own salvation. Let no one say that I discourage him, and propose to him a task beyond his own strength. All of us have the gifts of grace pledged to us from our youth up. We know this well; but we do not use our privilege. Narrow, indeed, is the way of life, but infinite is His love and power who is with the Church, in Christ's place, to guide us along it.'

Newman's sometimes over-severe teaching is tempered by this strong and living conviction of the assistance of the Holy Spirit, who, according to the Church's teaching throughout the ages, is the sanctifier par excellence. Three years later, in his sermon on 'Mental Prayer', he develops this theme still further. 'Never,' he writes, 'must it be supposed . . . that the gift of grace which we receive at baptism is a mere outward privilege. . . . This would be a gross and false view of the nature of God's mercy given us in Christ. For the new birth of the Holy Spirit sets the soul in motion in a heavenly way: it gives us good thoughts and desires, enlightens and purifies us, and prompts us to seek God. In a word . . . it gives a spiritual *life*; it opens the eyes of our mind, so that we begin to see God in all things by faith, and hold continual intercourse with Him by prayer; and if we cherish these gracious influences, we shall become holier and wiser and more heavenly, year by year. . . .'

We see how powerful Newman believed the influence of the Spirit to be. Though he insisted on a very austere morality, the spirituality he taught was no dry doctrine of virtues and vices, but an inner life guided by the Spirit and opening up new senses, the 'eyes of the soul' or 'the inward sight and taste' as he expressed it in the sermon quoted before—an idea very prominent in the Greek Fathers, especially Origen, from whom he had no doubt taken it over.

Newman's teaching on the indwelling Spirit was further developed in his *Lectures on Justification*, published in 1838. In these Lectures he attacked the Lutheran doctrine of justification by a merely external imputation of the merits of Christ as it was taught by contemporary Low Church Evangelicals and Nonconformists.

E

Newman repudiated this teaching as opposed to both Scripture and the doctrine of the universal Church. According to him justification, far from leaving the inner man as sinful as he had been before, was a true 'renewal', a 'wonderful grace of God, not in the heavens, but nigh to them (i.e. men), even in their mouth and in their heart'. 'Justification tends to sanctify; and to obstruct its sanctifying power, is as if we stopped a man's breath; it is the death of that from which it proceeds.' This justification 'is wrought by the power of the Spirit, or rather by His presence within us', and, he concludes: '*This* is to be justified, to receive the Divine Presence within us, and be made a Temple of the Holy Ghost.'

In describing this divine Presence, Newman reaches truly mystical heights. 'It would seem,' he says in the same Lectures, 'that, in truth, the principle of our spiritual existence is divine, is an ineffable presence of God. Christ, who promised to make all His disciples one in God with Him, who promised that we should be in God and God in us, has made us so—has in some mysterious way accomplished for us this great work, this stupendous privilege. It would seem, moreover . . . that He has done so by ascending to the Father; that His ascent bodily is His descent spiritually; that His taking our nature up to God, is the descent of God into us; that He has truly, though in an unknown sense, taken us to God, brought down God to us, according as we view it. Thus, when St Paul says that our life is hid with Him in God, we may suppose him to intimate that our principle of existence is no longer a mortal, earthly principle, such as Adam's after his fall, but that we are baptized and hidden anew in God's glory, in that Shekinah* of light and purity which we lost when Adam fell— that we are new-created, transformed, spiritualized, glorified in the Divine Nature—that through the participation of Christ, we receive, as through a channel, the true Presence of God within and without us, imbuing us with sanctity and immortality. *This* . . . is our justification, our ascent through Christ to God, or God's descent through Christ to us; we may call it either of the two;

---

* A term used in later Judaism, designating God's visible presence among men.

we ascend into Him, He descends into us; we are in Him, He in us; Christ being the One Mediator, the way, the truth, and the life, joining earth with heaven.'

I have quoted this passage at length, because here we see the other side of his spirituality, no longer the austere preaching of exalted virtue, but the awareness of the union of Christ with the believer, the indwelling of the divine Shekinah justifying, sanctifying and indeed glorifying the true Christian. When he did not directly address a congregation Newman's preoccupation with sin and its dire consequences receded into the background and he allowed the spiritual theologian to have the word. For Newman's was a many-sided personality, in this also resembling the Fathers of the Church, who were preachers, mystics, speculative theologians all in one, whereas in later times, especially after the thirteenth century, there was an increasing specialization; biblical exegesis, speculative and moral theology became ever more divorced from each other and from mystical theology, to the great disadvantage of each. Only in our own time, with the Second Vatican Council, have there been made persistent and already fruitful efforts to co-ordinate these different departments of Christian learning; and it is hardly an exaggeration to say that Newman has been the father of this renewal.

For his spirituality was a spirituality of integration, in which sacramental and mystical theology were intimately bound up with each other and with Christian moral teaching. For him baptism, for example, was far more than a mere ceremony admitting to the Christian Church, as it was for so many of his contemporaries; he insisted repeatedly on the real 'regeneration' it brought about. 'Infants just baptized' he writes in the sermon on the Gift of the Spirit quoted before, are 'bright as the Cherubim, as flames of fire rising heavenward in sacrifice to God' through the regenerating power of the baptismal water. But this angelic state is transitory; as the baptized children grow up, the light that is in them must either increase or be dimmed, 'while of grown men the multitude, alas!' he continues, 'might show but fearful tokens that the Lord had once been among them, only here and there some scattered witnesses for Christ remaining, and they, too, seamed all over with the scars of sin'. However, above the multitude of unsatisfactory Christians there are the saints or, as Newman liked to call them, the 'consistent' Christians who live their faith to the full.

Newman's Ideal Christian

He has described them several times especially in his sermons, and these descriptions furnish a very detailed picture of his spiritual ideal. In a sermon preached in 1831 entitled 'The Spiritual Mind' he told his congregation: 'We must adore Christ as our Lord and Master, and love Him as our most gracious Redeemer. We must have a deep sense of our guilt, and of the difficulty of securing heaven; we must live as in His presence, daily pleading His cross and passion, thinking of His holy commandments, imitating his sinless pattern, and depending on the gracious aids of His Spirit . . . we must, for His sake, aim at a noble and unusual strictness of life, perfecting holiness in His fear, destroying our sins, mastering our whole soul, and bringing it into captivity to His law, denying ourselves lawful things . . . exercising a profound humility, and an unbounded, never-failing love, giving away much of our substance in religious and charitable works, and discountenancing and shunning irreligious men. This is to be a Christian; a gift . . . attainable only with fear and much trembling.' Anyone who falls short of this high ideal 'is in a peril so great and fearful, that I do not like to speak about it'. It is significant that he again insisted on 'shunning irreligious men', which would preclude all apostolic activity and is, moreover, not exactly in harmony with 'unbounded, never-failing love'. At that time Newman's was still an inward-looking spirituality, a spirituality of 'fear and trembling'; words that recall his Danish contemporary Søren Kierkegaard with whom, as will be seen later, he has a certain affinity. Strictness of life, holiness in fear and an overpowering awareness of the difficulty of reaching heaven are the characteristics of this spirituality.

In a much later sermon on Equanimity, preached in 1839, Newman describes as his model Christian one who 'is cheerful, easy, kind, gentle, courteous, candid, unassuming; has no pretence, no affectation, no ambition, no singularity; because he has neither hope nor fear about this world. He is serious, sober, discreet, grave, moderate, mild.' This Christian, however, is also almost a Stoic, for 'he will feel indifferent to the course of human affairs . . . the Christian has no keen expectations, no acute mortifications, he is beyond hopes and fears, suspense and jealousy'—a portrait that certainly does not fit the Christian saints, many of whom took an intense interest in human affairs—as, incidentally, Newman himself did—and who certainly had acute mortifications, being by no means beyond hopes or fears.

The picture of the ideal Christian that Newman traced at this time cannot be called very attractive. He himself admits as much when he writes in a Sermon on the 'Moral Effects of Communion with God' that 'they who take their portion with the Church, will seem, except in some remarkable cases, unamiable to the world'; and in another on 'Christ Hidden from the World', 'The holier a man is, the less he is understood by men of the world . . . those who serve the world will be blind to him, or scorn and dislike him'. But a great many of the saints have been very attractive to the world, indeed, we need only think of a Francis of Assisi or Teresa of Avila, who are greatly admired, even by unbelievers. It is precisely these saints who have been most successful in converting sinners and atheists. For something is lacking in Newman's descriptions of his ideal Christian. It is that joy, that exuberance of love which arises from the experienced union with Christ and makes the saint, for all his personal austerity, intensely attractive. It is a real paradox that Newman, who was himself so attractive especially to the young, should have preached such an all-but-joyless spirituality, which led him even to affirm, in his sermon on 'The Visible Church', that it is the rule of God's government 'to leave His servants few and solitary', and that 'it is a Christian characteristic to look back on former times', that the Christian does not live in the present—that is a characteristic of 'the man of this world', but in the past, that he takes no interest in the world.

Friendship

There is one subject, however, on which Newman is very 'human', and that is friendship. His view of it is also very different from that of certain Catholic saints and spiritual writers, who warn against what is technically called 'special friendships'. Newman himself had an exceptional gift for friendship and was throughout his life surrounded by men who were deeply devoted to him; in 1831 he preached a sermon on the Feast of St John the Evangelist, on the subject of 'Love of Relations and Friends'. I should like to quote this sermon rather extensively, not only because natural human friendship is sometimes considered detrimental to high sanctity, but also because what Newman says on this subject will show that he was actually far more understanding than some of his severe pronouncements, quoted above, may have led the reader to assume.

Commenting on Christ's special friendship for John, 'the beloved disciple', Newman affirms 'that there is nothing contrary to the spirit of the Gospel, nothing inconsistent with the fulness of Christian love, in having our affections directed in an especial way . . . towards those whom the circumstances of our past life, or some peculiarities of character, have endeared to us. There have been men before now, who have supposed Christian love was so diffusive as not to admit of concentration upon individuals; so that we ought to love all men equally. . . . Now I shall here maintain . . . that the best preparation for loving the world at large, and loving it duly and wisely, is to cultivate an intimate friendship and affection towards those who are immediately about us. . . . We are to begin with loving our friends about us, and gradually to enlarge the circle of our affections, till it reaches all Christians, and then all men. Besides, it is obviously impossible to love all men in any strict and true sense. What is meant by loving all men, is to feel well disposed to all men, to be ready to assist them. . . .

And love, besides, is a habit, and cannot be attained without actual *practice*, which on so large a scale is impossible. . . . The real love of man *must* depend on practice, and therefore must begin by exercising itself on our friends around us, otherwise it will have no existence. By trying to love our relations and friends, by submitting to their wishes, though contrary to our own, by bearing with their infirmities, by overcoming their occasional waywardness by kindness, by dwelling on their excellences, and trying to copy them, thus it is that we form in our hearts that root of charity, which, though small at first, may, like the mustard seed, at last even overshadow the earth.'

However much Newman may insist on self-denial, however high an ideal of virtue he may place before his hearers, he never forgets that man is a social being, that he does not live in a vacuum, and that only by cultivating natural love and friendship will he learn to love also supernaturally. The only time when we have to give up even this love for our relations and friends is if God himself should lead us 'by a strange way . . . and cast these objects of our earthly affection into the shade', then, 'they must, for the time, disappear from our hearts'.

How much Newman himself felt the need for friendship, and even at times for more than friendship, emerges from an entry in his diary in March 1840. There, after a detailed description of his illness in Sicily, he asks himself why he is writing all this. 'For myself, I may look at it once or twice in my whole life, and what sympathy is there in *my* looking at it? Whom have I, whom can I have, who would take interest in it? . . . This is the sort of interest which a wife takes and none but she—it is a woman's interest—and that interest, so be it, shall never be taken in me. . . . All my habits for years, my tendencies, are towards celibacy. I could not take that interest in this world which marriage requires. I am too disgusted with this world. . . . And therefore I willingly give up the possession of that sympathy, which I feel is not, cannot be, granted to me. Yet, not the less do I feel the need of it. Who will care to be told such details as I have put down above? Shall I ever have in my old age spiritual children who will take an interest such as a wife does? . . . What a dream is life. I used to regret festival days going quick. They are come and they are gone; but so it is, time is nothing except as the seed of eternity.'

Here the stern preacher reveals a very different side of himself, the longing of the man for intimate feminine understanding, which every celibate priest has to sacrifice. This sacrifice is perhaps even more difficult, especially in middle age, than the mere abstinence from sexual intercourse, and friendship is no sufficient equivalent. To be interested in the small worries, in a man's health, in his moods, in his material needs and well-being and to give him her sympathy and understanding in those intimate and private things unknown or unrevealed to the world at large—this is one of the most important offices of Eve the 'helpmate', and Newman was painfully aware of this unfulfilled need of his nature. But he made the sacrifice because he was convinced that God required it from him, though it would have been perfectly lawful for him, as a priest of the Church of England, to take a wife.

Humour

The austere teaching of his sermons and his 'disgust with the world' expressed in this passage as elsewhere in his earlier writings might give the impression that Newman was always serious. But this is far from being the case; he would not have attracted his young undergraduates so powerfully if he had been, and that he had a great sense of fun is proved by his correspondence. One example should suffice. He had a very 'spiky' curate, whose one great subject was the necessity of fasting. This is how Newman wrote about him in a letter to a friend: 'What does he do on St Michael's day but preach a sermon, not simply on angels, but on his one subject, for which he has a monomania, of fasting; nay, and say that it was a good thing, whereas angels feasted on festivals, to make the brute creation fast on fast days: so I am told. May he (*salvis ossibus suis*, [i.e. saving his bones]) have a fasting horse the next time he goes steeple-chasing.' Nevertheless in the

Church of England of his time Newman was constantly trying to combat the superficiality of a religion of 'All things bright and beautiful', as the popular hymn has it, and this led him to place at times exaggerated emphasis on the severer side of Christian teaching.

Imitating Christ

Again, in opposition to the emotionalism of Evangelicals and the Free Churches, he preached a spirituality very much opposed to the emotions, for, he wrote in his sermon on 'The Humiliations of the Eternal Son', 'the so-called religion of the heart, without orthodoxy of doctrine, is but the warmth of a corpse, real for a time, but sure to fail'. Moreover, his view of Christ prevented him from attributing any strong feelings to him. 'Can we find anywhere,' he asked in his sermon on 'Religious Emotion', 'such calmness and simplicity as marked His devotion and His obedience? When does He ever speak with fervour or vehemence?' Here Scripture itself contradicts Newman. For surely the great woes Jesus pronounced over the scribes and Pharisees were spoken with considerable emotion, and when he drove the moneychangers from the Temple he can hardly be said not to have shown any 'vehemence'. When he raised Lazarus he was 'deeply moved in spirit and troubled', and when he prayed in the garden St Matthew's Gospel says that 'he began to be sorrowful and troubled', while St Luke even attributes 'sweat . . . like great drops of blood' to him. Here Newman simply fails to take account of the facts that are opposed to his views, but goes by his own feelings, because 'to suppose otherwise' he writes, 'were an irreverence towards Him'.

Hence, as Christians ought to imitate Christ they, too, must preserve perfect calm in their religion. Indeed, as he says in his sermon on 'Religious Worship', 'Men who have grown up in the faith and fear of God, have a calm and equable piety; so much so that they are often charged on that very account with being dull, cold, formal, insensible.' It can hardly be said of a St Bernard or a St John of the Cross that they appeared dull, cold or formal. It may, however, be admitted that the religion of the Book of Common Prayer, on which Newman's spirituality was naturally nourished, does not encourage mystical transports; as he himself says in his sermon on 'Religious Emotion' mentioned before : 'You will look in vain in the Prayer Book for long or vehement prayers; for it is only upon occasions that agitation of mind is right, but there is ever a call upon us for seriousness, gravity, simplicity, deliberate trust, deep-seated humility.'

Through Obedience

It is in keeping with this image of the perfect Christian that the virtue on which Newman insists most often is obedience. By obedience Newman does not mean obedience to a religious superior or spiritual guide, the sense attached to the word by most spiritual writers, whether Roman or Anglo-Catholic. For Newman obedience is given either directly to God or through the mediation of Scripture. In his sermon on 'Faith and Obedience' he defines it as 'the obvious mode, suggested by nature, of a creature's conducting himself in God's sight, who fears Him as his Maker, and knows that, as a sinner, he has especial cause for fearing Him'. Hence he will look for the best means of propitiating God, 'and he will find nothing better as an offering, or as an evidence, than obedience to that Holy Law, which conscience tells him has been given us by God Himself'.

In his second University Sermon Newman introduces obedience into his definition of Religion, which he calls 'the system of relations existing between us and a Supreme Power, claiming our habitual obedience', and in his Lectures on Justification he identifies it with the 'renewal of mind' by which we are justified, for 'though justification properly means an act external to us, it may be said to consist in evangelical obedience'; hence it is not surprising that he should tell his congregation, in his sermon on 'The Strictness of the Law of Christ', preached in 1837, that 'till we aim at complete, unreserved obedience in all things, we are not really

Christians at all'. Newman does not go into any details; he does not discuss the innumerable situations in every human life where it is very difficult to decide what exactly 'evangelical obedience' demands in these particular circumstances; but in his sermon on the feast of St John the Evangelist, preached in 1831, he ennunciates one strange principle, namely of 'dislike of change being not only the characteristic of a virtuous mind, but in some sense a virtue itself'. Here, again, Newman was preaching himself, for his own dislike of change went so far as to include even foreign travel; he was happiest in his room at Oriel 'sporting his oak'.* He called it 'a sordid, narrow, miserable ambition to attempt to *leave* our earthly lot; to be wearied or ashamed of what we are, to hanker after . . . novelty of life'; for as he said in his sermon on 'Doing Glory to God in Pursuits of the World', following the Prayer Book, 'The Lord Jesus Christ our Saviour is best served . . . when men . . . do their duty in that state of life in which it has pleased God to call them', a view which also made him averse to democracy.

Newman rings the changes on this subject of obedience, which he calls 'the highest glory' of creatures. 'Any obedience,' he says in his sermon on 'Watching', 'is better than none—any profession which is disjoined from obedience, is a mere pretence and deceit. . . . Obedience is the only way of seeking Him. All your duties are obediences. If you are to believe the truths He has revealed, to regulate yourselves by His precepts, to be frequent in His ordinances, to adhere to His Church and people, why is it, except because *He* has bid you? And to do what He bids is to obey Him, and to obey Him is to approach Him. Every act of obedience is an approach—an approach to Him who is not far off, though He seems so, but close behind this visible screen of things which hides Him from us.'

In his earlier sermons, Newman preached obedience much more than love, though obedience is certainly inseparable from love, as Christ himself said : 'If you love me, you will keep my commandments.' Again, this stress on obedience rather than on love

* Locking the outer door.

was caused by the easy-going religion of his time in which feelings of love and devotion played a central part. It is significant that the further he moved away from his own reactions against contemporary religion the more he insisted on love. Thus, in a sermon on 'The New Works of the Gospel', preached in 1840 he contradicted what he himself had said three years earlier, namely that 'any obedience is better than none', and taught that 'Our best obedience in our strength is worth nothing . . . not only so, it is the obedience of souls born and living under God's wrath, for a state of nature is a state of wrath. On the other hand, obedience which is done in faith is done with the aid of the Holy Spirit', and a year before he had preached on 'Love, the One Thing needful' saying that 'even strict obedience is no evidence of fervent love'.

Summing Up

From what has been said Newman's spiritual teaching during the heyday of the Oxford Movement may seem somewhat negative. His pessimism, his deep conviction of man's natural depravity and the dire consequences of sin even in the converted give it an appearance of gloom that was shared also by the other protagonists of the Movement, Keble and especially Pusey. The latter even went so far as to consider a smile incompatible with the seriousness of the exemplary Christian, except when talking to children. That the severity of his preaching was only partly in keeping with Newman's character is evident from his letters, which are often full of excitement and certainly not always without sarcastic asides. Though people loved and venerated him, he wrote of himself in a letter to an admiring lady: 'I am *not* venerable, and nothing can make me so. I am very much like other people, and I do not think it necessary to abstain from the feelings and thoughts, not intrinsically sinful, which other people have. I cannot speak words of wisdom: to some it comes naturally . . . I have never been in office of station, people have never bowed to me, and I could not endure it. I tell you frankly, my infirmity, I believe, is always to be rude to persons who are deferential in manner to me.'

That Newman was 'very much like other people' is certainly not quite true, and he was himself not nearly so forbidding as the religion he preached. But then this religion of the *Via Media* was a very personal religion; produced from an individual interpretation of the Fathers and the Bible; it could of its nature only be the religion of the few, and for this very reason it was not the religion of the Christian Church, which was meant for all men, not only for an élite—this is another trait it shares with Jansenism. But that it was a religion for an élite is quite clear from the tremendous impression it made on a very large circle of men and women who represented all that was most spiritual in contemporary Anglicanism. To quote only one letter from a stranger when the rumour spread, in 1844, that Newman was about to join the Catholic Church: 'Your published *Parochial Sermons* have been, under God, the means of rousing me from spiritual sleep, and I have from them, and from their operation upon my mind, been led to regard your opinions with a reverence greater than I can express.' For the Church of England had, indeed, been spiritually asleep— it was Newman who was at the centre of the movement that aroused it from this sleep. His sermons brought his hearers into contact with the living God of the Bible, the God who demanded their wholehearted obedience and surrender. When they listened to him they were aware that here was a man of complete sincerity who spoke not about things he had read in books but about what he had deeply experienced in his own life, a man for whom the doctrines of the Christian Church were the truths revealed by God on whose acceptance depended their salvation.

These doctrines, however, were not those of Protestantism, of Luther and Calvin, they were neither justification by faith alone nor predistination to heaven or hell; they were instead the doctrines of the early Church as represented in the Creeds, including the so-called Athanasian Creed with its elaborate definitions of the Trinity and the Incarnate Son of God and its affirmation that those who do not hold this Catholic faith cannot be saved. Moreover, from 1839 Newman had come to have doubts about the

Catholicity of the Church of England which he could only over-come by giving a 'Catholic' interpretation to the Thirty-Nine Articles which every clergyman had to sign. These doubts led to the publication of the famous *Tract 90*, which introduced that period in Newman's life when he came to be torn between his loyalty to the Church in which he had been brought up and his increasing conviction that this Church was not the same as the Church of the Fathers.

4 ON HIS WAY TO THE CATHOLIC CHURCH

NEWMAN's first serious doubts that the Church of England was the Catholic Church or even a branch of it began in 1839. He had been studying the history of the Council of Chalcedon (451 A.D.), when, as he writes in a letter of July 1839 to his friend F. Rogers, two things struck him as very remarkable, 'the great power of the Pope (as great as he claims now almost), and the marvellous interference of the civil power, as great almost as in our kings'. Two months later he received what he called in a letter to the same correspondent 'the first real hit from Romanism'. This came from an article by Dr Wiseman, the later Cardinal-Archbishop of Westminster, in the *Dublin Review* of August of that year. So far Newman had judged both the Church of England and the Church of Rome by the standard of antiquity. He had always used the same terms of reference as the great seventeenth century Anglicans, who relied on the writings of the Fathers of the first centuries and considered that the Church of Rome had made extraneous additions to the ancient creeds. But in the article of Wiseman he found that St Augustine himself had used another criterion for the true faith, namely the principle: *Securus judicat orbis terrarum*, meaning that the judgement of the whole Church is safe, or, as Newman expresses it, 'that the deliberate judgement, in which the whole Church at length rests and acquiesces, is an infallible prescription . . . the words of St Augustine struck me with a power which I never had felt from any words before . . . the theory of *Via Media* was absolutely pulverized'.

In the spring of 1839 his influence in the Anglican Church had been at its height. He had, as he himself acknowledged, 'supreme

79

confidence in my controversial *status*, and I had a great and still growing success, on recommending it to others'. Now the first great breach had been made in this confidence. His only consolation was that grace might be given even in a schismatical Church, and so, as he wrote in yet another letter to Mr Rogers, in October, he considered that a Church that had broken away from the centre of unity might put herself into 'a state of penance' and that her children would be 'best fulfilling their duty to her—not by leaving her, but by promoting her return'.

After the first excitement these considerations had caused him Newman settled down to study the matter still further and came to the conclusion that though the Church of England might be in schism, the Church of Rome, on the other hand, practised what looked like idolatry; hence he remained content to stay where he was and to advise others, who became unsettled, to do likewise.

At the same time his own spiritual life as well as his teaching were led into increasingly 'Catholic' channels. In March 1838 he had heard a confession for the first time. For a Catholic priest hearing confessions is, of course, part of the vocation for which he has been trained; for Newman it was a great event in his life, so that it is not surprising that he should have told the young man who asked him that he felt it painful, 'both from the responsibility and the distressing trial of hearing it'. During Lent of the following year he observed very stringent rules of fasting and abstinence, in imitation of the early Fathers, on Wednesdays and Fridays not breaking his fast till five o'clock in the evening. On the Ember Days of September he found to his surprise that he could fast till the evening without any inconvenience, concluding the entry in his diary: 'Gratias tibi Domine—whither art Thou leading me?' In 1840 he increased his Lenten penances, refraining also from wearing gloves, and he used the Roman Breviary services for his devotions.

Throughout these years, he not only continued to preach at St Mary's, but he also did more and more pastoral work at the church at Littlemore, which at that time belonged to the living of St Mary's. Nevertheless, his position at the university church was becoming difficult owing to the indiscretion of one of his curates who preached there 'the Roman doctrine of the Mass'. Newman himself had introduced weekly communion, which was well attended, especially by graduates of the University. At Littlemore, however, he had to cope with very different problems, which show him in a rather unusual light. For there he had to catechize the school children, and in the process he had 'been reforming, or at least lecturing against uncombed hair and dirty faces and hands; but I find I am not deep in the philosophy of school-girl tidiness'. Nevertheless, a few weeks later he could report to his sister that he had 'effected a great reform (for the time) in the girls' hands and faces. Lectured with unblushing effrontery on the necessity of their keeping their work clean, and set them to knit stockings.'

For, strange though it may seem in an intellectual like Newman, he had his practical side as well and was able to cope with whatever was needed at the moment. There is hardly a better example of the versatility and adaptability of his mind than that he could so well clarify Christian doctrine for the ignorant small girls of Littlemore that one of his friends who had gone out to hear him wrote home: 'Newman's catechizing has been a great attraction this Lent, and men have gone out of Oxford every Sunday to hear it. I heard him last Sunday, and thought it very striking, done with such spirit, and the children so up to it, answering with the greatest alacrity.'

At the same time he also had to undertake a certain amount of spiritual direction, an activity hardly practised at all in the contemporary Church of England. A lady who had recently been impressed by his writings and the spirituality of the Tracts desired to help by publishing some work of her own. Newman rejected this idea, advising that she should 'employ herself in her own edification. Let her turn her activity and energy upon herself; let her consider how much must be done by every one of us to enter life, how much is open to every one to do, both to the glory of God, and towards personal improvement; how high and wonderful a thing Christian Sanctity is, and what capabilities the regenerate

F

soul has for improvement. The talents which she possesses admit
under God's grace of indefinite improvement and confirmation,
and may be blessed by Him for securing to her a place among the
Saints.' He then advised her to study the *Imitation of Christ*,
Pascal's *Thoughts*, the devotional writings of Jeremy Taylor, and
the lives of the saints, and to say the Breviary, 'with such omissions as the English Church requires'. As his thoughts at this time
ran also on the advantages of re-establishing the monastic life in
the Church of England, he further advised her to pray for 'a life
of such observances, like the saints of old'.

As happens so often after a conspicuous conversion, this lady,
who is called 'Miss H.' in the correspondence published by Anne
Mozley, wanted to do great things for God and make certain
vows, which Newman had to discourage, because, as he wrote to
her, 'there is great danger of any one who has experienced such
a change of views as the writer of the letter, becoming excited'.
And he goes on to warn that 'she must not expect to have always
the sunshine she has now, and the more she indulges her feelings
now, the greater reverse perhaps is in store'. Here he draws on
the common experience of all Christians who give themselves
sincerely to prayer that the spiritual life is full of vicissitudes, that
periods of great religious fervour are inevitably followed by dryness and even disgust for spiritual activities. Evidently something
like this did happen to Miss H., for a month later Newman has
to tell her that 'No one must be surprised, particularly when first
making an effort to live strictly, at discouragement, failures, and
the apparent hopelessness of making progress. You must not
mind these things—everybody experiences the like. You must not
be impatient nor over-anxious, but go steadily on, feeling thankful
that you have, please, God, time before you. . . . You can but do
God's will, as far as may be, according to your day, and leave the
whole matter to Him.'

Soon Miss H.'s troubles seem to have become worse, because
she evidently confessed to doubts. Newman's answer is very significant, for it deals with a problem that had long been in his mind
and to which he later was to devote a whole book (The *Grammar*

of Assent). 'Be assured,' he writes to Miss H., 'that I have my doubts and difficulties as other people. Perhaps the more we examine and investigate, the more we have to perplex us. It is the lot of man: the human mind in its present state is unequal to its own powers of comprehension; it embraces more than it can master. I think we ought all to set out on our enquiries, I am sure we shall end them, with this conviction. Absolute certainty, then, cannot be attained here; we must resign ourselves to doubt as the *trial under* which it is God's will we should do our duty and prepare ourselves for His presence. Our sole question must be, *what* does a merciful God, who knows whereof we are made, wish *us to do under* our existing ignorance and doubt?'

Newman did not, could not teach a cut and-dried faith unperturbed by any difficulty. As his early evangelicalism was being replaced by an increasingly Catholic outlook, the problems of modern thought made themselves felt more powerfully. Faith was not something you could prove to your own satisfaction and then possess like a piece of clothing or furniture. Faith was a venture; it involved a risk. As early as 1834 he had preached a sermon on 'Faith without Sight' in which he had said that 'If it is but fairly probable that rejection of the Gospel will involve his eternal ruin, it is safest and wisest to act as if it were certain'. Two years later, in another sermon, called 'The Ventures of Faith', he taught that, since according to the Letter to the Hebrews 'faith is the assurance of things hoped for, the conviction of things not seen', it 'is in its very essence the making present what is unseen; the acting upon the mere prospect of it, as if it really were possessed; the venturing upon it, the staking present ease, happiness, or other good, upon the chance of the future'. Hence he continues, 'it follows that our duty lies in risking upon Christ's word what we have, for what we have not'. And in 1840, the year in which the letters to Miss H. were written, he returned to the subject even more forcefully in a sermon significantly entitled 'Subjection of the Reason and Feelings to the Revealed Word'. There he says that 'Faith outstrips argument. If there is only a fair chance that the Bible is true, that heaven is the reward of obedience, and hell of wilful sin, it is worth while, it is safe, to sacrifice this world to the next. It were worth while, though Christ told us to sell all that we have and follow Him, and to pass our time here in poverty and contempt, it were worth while on that chance to do it.' And in his University Sermon on 'Love the Safeguard of Faith against Superstition' he writes that 'Faith ventures and hazards; right Faith ventures and hazards deliberately, seriously, soberly, piously, and humbly, counting the cost and delighting in the sacrifice'.

Now this idea of faith as a venture, a hazard rather than a safe possession, was not new. Pascal had elaborated it in his famous simile of the wager in the *Thoughts,* which Newman recommended to Miss H. There the French philosopher had written that reason could not determine whether God exists or not—a view quite different from that of the medieval scholastics who affirmed that His existence could be rationally proved—that man must choose between the two—and he proceeded to show that it was reasonable to opt for God's existence. For, he argued, if you wager that God exists and He does exist, you gain all because you gain infinite beatitude; if He does not, you lose nothing. Therefore, he concludes, 'our proposition is of infinite force, because we risk the finite in a game where there is an equal chance of gain or loss, and with infinity to gain'.

Newman's contemporoay Søren Kierkegaard based his theology on a similar thought; though he brought into it the element of '*Angst*', the anguish caused by man's freedom of choice which makes him acquainted with sin and brings him to the point of despair. There, in the grip of *Angst,* he must make his final choice, for or against God, and this choice is no longer conditioned by argument, as in Pascal, but it is a 'leap' into faith by which we lay hold of God through personal choice.

Newman, like Pascal, asked his disciples to risk the seen for the unseen, for, as he writes in his *Essay on the Development of Christian Doctrine,* 'it is safer to believe' and that the reasons for believing consist 'rather of presumptions and ventures after the truth than of accurate and complete proofs'. For him, however, the 'risk' was not so much for or against the existence of God; for

* utmost bliss

since his experience as a boy of fifteen he had been aware of himself and God as the only two self-evident beings; for him faith introduces 'to the unseen Presence of God', and the venture of faith consists 'in risking upon Christ's word what we have for what we have not'. The risk for him involves the whole of the Gospel, the truth of what the Bible teaches. Soon he was himself to be called to 'risk' his whole existence on what he had come to believe was the true Church.

But before he was called upon to make this choice he had himself to pass through much pain and anguish. In the same year (1840) in which he had told Miss H. that he himself had doubts and difficulties he resolved to help others to disperse them by writing a Tract, the famous number 90, on the Catholic interpretation of the Thirty-Nine Articles. His object in writing the tract was to show that, whatever the intention of the Protestant authors of the articles might have been, they ought to be interpreted not in the sense of the authors, but according to the mind of the Catholic Church. With enormous erudition Newman compared the Articles with the doctrine of the Council of Trent as well as with the Anglican Book of Homilies and a wealth of other relevant material, concluding that 'The Protestant Confession was drawn up with the purpose of including Catholics; and Catholics now will not be excluded. What was an economy* in the Reformers, is a protection to us. What would have been a perplexity to us then, is a perplexity to Protestants now. We could not then have found fault with their voice; they cannot now repudiate our meaning.'

The Tract was published at the beginning of March 1841. Its devastating effect took Newman completely by surprise. On March 9 he wrote to his sister that he had 'just published a Tract which I did not feel likely to attract attention. . . . But people are taking it up very warmly', and three days later : 'I fear I am clean dished. The Heads of Houses are at this very moment concocting a manifesto against me.' The controversy that followed made Newman's

---

* In the sense of 'judicious handling of doctrine', according to the Oxford English Dictionary.

position in the Church of England increasingly difficult. Here we are only concerned with the spiritual causes and effects of Tract and controversy. Its causes are set out by Newman in the Letter he wrote to his bishop in his defence: 'Our business is with ourselves,' he writes, 'to make ourselves more holy, more self-denying, more primitive, more worthy of our high calling. . . . While I have considered that we ought to be content with the outward circumstances in which Providence has placed us, I have tried to feel that the great business of one and all of us is, to endeavour to raise the moral tone of the Church. It is sanctity of heart and conduct which commends us to God. If we be holy, all will go well with us.'

Holiness was the object of Newman's preaching, holiness that of the Tracts—but holiness could only be learned from the Fathers and the early traditions of the Church, not, he felt, from the teaching of the Reformers.

Newman's opponents cared little for his motives. They saw only one thing in *Tract 90*: its defence of many Catholic teachings and practices abhorrent to staunch Protestants, and hence they regarded it as an unmistakable signpost in the direction of Rome. The heads of the Oxford colleges were against him, but his own bishop, a not very energetic man who preferred peace to controversy, contented himself with asking him to discontinue the tracts and considering No. 90 objectionable not on doctrinal grounds but 'as tending to disturb the Church'. Newman was happy that there had been no dogmatic condemnation, for, as he characteristically observed in a letter to Keble, 'I cannot be a demagogue or a quasi-schismatic'.

After this upheaval Newman spent the summer in retreat at Littlemore, occupied with translating St Athanasius. But what had promised to be a period of scholarly calm turned into more interior unrest. For now his studies led him to realize that the Church of England was not in the position of the Catholics defended by Athanasius, but in that of the unorthodox semi-Arians supported by the Byzantine government. Moreover, though his own bishop had been satisfied with his explanations, others began to deliver 'charges' against him, which made it unpleasantly clear that their views of the Church of England were very different from his, so that he could not but admit to his friend, J. R. Hope: 'that the said Charges are very serious matters; as virtually silencing portions of the truth in particular dioceses, and as showing that it is not impossible that our Church *may* lapse into heresy. I cannot deny that a great and anxious *experiment* is going on, whether our Church be or be not Catholic; the issue may not be in our day. But I must be plain in saying that, if it does issue in Protestantism, I shall think it my duty, if alive, to leave it. . . . I fear I must say that I am beginning to think that the only way to keep in the English Church is steadily to contemplate and act upon the possibility of leaving it.'

Newman's anxieties were increased by the affair of the Jerusalem bishopric, about which he heard in October. This was a purely political move to increase British influence in Palestine. France and Russia were the official protectors of Catholic and Greek Orthodox interests in the Middle East, and in order to counteract their influence England and Prussia determined to set up a bishopric in Jerusalem to cater for any Protestants, converted Jews and minor Eastern sects as well as for a handful of Anglicans. Newman was horrified at this mix-up of denominations. 'The Archbishop is doing all he can to unchurch us,' he wrote to his sister Jemima, and to Keble: 'So we join with Protestant Prussia to found a sect, and put a Bishop over it.' 'Is all this the way to keep certain of our members from Rome? or is it on the whole desirable that they should go, and a good riddance?' he asked in an unpublished letter to *The Times*.

He himself was not yet ready to go, for he was too profoundly convinced that a change of religion was a step that ought to be taken only after a preparation of many years. But the letters of this period show how profoundly uneasy he had by now become about the catholicity of the Church of England; for he felt that his 'opinions went far beyond what had been customary in the English Church. . . . I have had many schemes floating on my mind how to get out of a position which of all is to me most odious

—that of a teacher setting up for himself against authority.'

At the end of the year, in November and December 1841, he preached four sermons at St Mary's for those who had become unsettled in the Church of England by the recent events. The gist of them was that, though the outward signs of the Church such as unity and Catholicity had been obscured in the Church of England, there was nevertheless sufficient evidence of a more private and inward nature that Christ had not forsaken it. At the same time these sermons show what the Church of England had done for his own spiritual life. 'If,' he adjures his hearers, 'you have gained any good thing, not merely in, but through your Church; if you have come to Service, and been favoured with the peace or the illumination you needed; or if you can recollect times when you visited holy places, and certainly gained there a manifestation such as the world could not give . . . or if your soul has been, as it were, transfigured within you, when you came to the Most Holy Sacrament; or if Lent and Passiontide brought to you what you had not before . . . or if you have experience of death-beds, and know how full of hope the children of our Church can die— O! pause ere you doubt that we have a Divine Presence among us still, and have not to seek it.'

These are the anguished words of a man who can no longer really believe in his own Church and yet cannot refuse to admit that he has received great graces from it. Nevertheless, the odds against the national Church are heavy. For 'we English . . . have, not one, but a hundred gospels among ourselves . . . till our very note and symbol is discord, and we wrangle and denounce, and call it life; but peace we know not, nor faith, nor love'. 'Who' therefore, 'can be startled, not I, if a person here or there . . . leaves us for some other communion?' Yet again, he feels that Anglicans are in a peculiar way attached to their Church; this he thinks, must be the work of angels: 'Angels surely stand in our way, in mercy, not in wrath; Angels warn us back. Let us obey the warning.' In the next sermon he reverts to the idea of interior evidence; 'religious men,' he says, 'have in their own religiousness, an evidence of the truth of their religion.' They may not be able to argue about it, but there are 'inward effects . . . which guarantee to a man the divinity of his form of religion, which make him willing to risk his salvation upon it'. Here we have again the element of 'risk', this very personal, existential stake in religion which is its life. But what if we can no longer take this risk? At the end of the fourth of these sermons Newman asks: 'What want we then but faith in our Church? with faith we can do every thing; without faith we can do nothing. If we have a secret misgiving about her, all is lost; we lose our nerve, our powers, our position, our hope.'

Thus Newman sought to convince himself and others that the Church of England was at least a branch of the Catholic and Apostolic Church. But these sermons give one rather the impression of a child singing in the dark because he is afraid. Newman tried desperately to convince others, because he himself was no longer convinced. On Christmas Day he wrote to a friend 'that our Church has through centuries ever been sinking lower and lower, till a good part of its pretensions and professions is a mere sham, though it be a duty to make the best of what we have received'. At the beginning of the following year he had come to the conclusion that his preaching at St Mary's had become 'a cause of irritation', and mid-February he removed himself and his books to Littlemore, where he had bought some cottages, and spent a very austere Lent, though he had to allow himself some relaxations so as not to damage his health. Nevertheless, he did not yet give up St Mary's but in the same year still preached some of his most powerful sermons there.

The subject of four of them, delivered towards the end of the year, was again the Church; but this time not the Church of England, but the Church of Christ as a power, a kingdom with its own unifying organization. 'If we will be scriptural in our view of the Church,' he tells his congregation, 'we must consider that it is a kingdom, that its officers have great powers and high gifts, that they are charged with the custody of Divine Truth, that they are all united together, and that the nations are subject to them. If we reject this kind of ministry, as inapplicable to the present day, we shall in vain go to Scripture to find another. If we will form to ourselves a ministry and a Church bereft of the august power which I have mentioned, it will be one of our own devising; and let us pretend no more to draw our religion from the Bible.'

It must have been difficult for his hearers to recognize the Church of England in this description; it corresponded so much more closely to the Church of Rome. For Newman continued to tell them that this kingdom 'occupied ground; it claimed to rule over those whom hitherto this world's governments ruled over without rival; and if this world's governments would not themselves acknowledge and submit to its rule, and rule under and according to its laws, it "broke in pieces" those governments'—surely a description that fitted none but the Catholic Church of later Christian antiquity and the middle ages.

Nevertheless, external power was not the main sign of the true Church, that sign was sanctity. 'Power and influence,' he wrote in another of this series of sermons, 'and credit, and authority, and wealth flow into her, because she does not ask for them : she has, because she does not seek : but let her seek them, and she loses them. . . . For when men see disinterested goodness, and holiness which has no selfish aims . . . and faith which sacrifices this world for the next, they cannot help giving to those who display these excellences that which such persons are content to lose, and for which they ask not—credit and influence. . . . The Saints live in sackcloth, and they are buried in silk and jewels. The Church refuses the gifts of this world, but these gifts come to her unbidden. Power, and influence, and credit, and authority, and wealth flow into her, because she does not ask for them.'

Thus Newman combines the spiritual signs of the Church, especially her sanctity as exemplified in the lives of the best of her children, with the external power and influence that she must also necessarily possess in order to fulfil her vocation on earth. But again, such a description of a Church, both spiritual and world-governing did not fit the Church to which he still belonged, and he himself became increasingly aware of it. Yet he was still waiting for guidance, for, as he wrote in a sermon preached about the same time: 'For His call you must wait—whether He will call you forward in your present state of life, or call you to change it.'

Lent of the following year, spent again at Littlemore in the company of some friends, was devoted not only to physical penance, but also included seven days' retreat during which they made formal meditation according to the method of the founder of the Jesuits, St Ignatius of Loyola. Newman's notes of this week of intense prayer and self-analysis throw a revealing light on his own spiritual development during this crucial period of his life. Though he had, of course, been accustomed to daily prayers from his youth, the idea of an hour's meditation at a time had been foreign to him and he had actually been afraid beforehand that he would not know what to do. The subject of the first meditation was that men are created to serve God, and this led him to a searching self-examination during which he accused himself of hardly ever having acted for God's glory, 'that my motive in all my exertions during the last ten years, has been the pleasure of energizing intellectually, as if my talents were given me to play a game with . . . that Selflove in one shape or another, e.g. vanity, desire of the good opinion of friends, etc. have been my motive, and that possibly it is *the* sovereign sin in my heart'.

A moral theologian would probably say that what Newman here calls sin is not sin but temptation. Again, just as he was terrified of his ambition as a young undergraduate, Newman became aware of the dangers of his great intellect, dangers which had been intensified by the enormous reputation he had gained in Oxford and indeed throughout England and beyond, and the wholehearted admiration and devotion of his friends. Moreover, all creative work—as opposed to other forms of work—whatever the discipline or even the suffering that may accompany it, has a joy inherent in itself and gives a satisfaction that cannot always be distinguished from self-satisfaction. The priest-theologian who works for God can hardly help feeling satisfied when he realizes that his writings have brought people nearer to God, when his sermons have converted sinners, or even when he has worked out solutions for intricate problems. The difficulty is whether the prime motive of his work is to enhance his own reputation or his devotion to the cause of Christianity. Newman was not sure about this, and indeed it was scarcely possible that he could be, because so far he had not been tried in the crucible of failure.

During his second exercise he had to endure trials quite common in meditation; but these were his first efforts, made without an adviser who could have reassured him, and so they troubled him a good deal. It may, however, be encouraging to others that even a spiritual giant like Newman was afflicted with such ordinary defects as wandering thoughts and sleepiness, and that far from being prepared to suffer dire tortures and undergo a thousand deaths in the service of his Master, as we have read in so many lives of the saints and mystics, he confessed that 'various great trials stuck me: 1. the having to make a General Confession to some one in our Church, I not having full faith that our Church has the power of Absolution. 2. having to join the Church of Rome. 3. having to give up my Library. 4. bodily pain and hardship. I considered that God is used to accept offers, but I trust He will not exact such.'

It would have been quite unreal for an Oxford don of the nineteenth century to have imagined being burned to death or broken by torture; he reflected on trials that might actually come to him, which may seem slight to our generation who have been inured to concentration camps and atom bombs, but which were the only real sufferings he could think of, and it is heartening for us that he shrank as much as any ordinary mortal from 'bodily pain and hardship', trusting that God would not inflict these on him, and that one of the worst trials he could imagine was being deprived of his books. God did not ask these things from him—but he did ask him to join the Church of Rome, as became increasingly clear.

The second day of his retreat was devoted to meditations on sin. 'Though the subject was so full of topics ("my sins"),' he writes, 'yet I seemed unable to interest or engage my mind', which is not surprising. For a well-balanced man like Newman unused as he was to 'examinations of conscience' which are a matter of course to Catholics, it cannot have been very profitable to make his own sins a subject of meditation, and he wandered off into such strange thoughts as 'how dreadful it would be to confess to this person or that'.

This matter of confession became a real problem to him, owing on the one hand to a certain very natural reluctance to admit humiliating faults, and on the other to the general lack of the practice of confession in the Church of England of his time, which made it such a far more personal and upsetting affair than in the Catholic Church where it is practised from childhood. However, Newman set out resolutely to rid himself of his weakness and decided in the course of his meditation 'to confess to L. that I just now, in excuse for omitting to read out aloud something from Stone [the meditation book they were using], said that I thought it came after Compline, whereas in fact I forgot it'. It was certainly a very minor fault; but it shows how difficult Newman found it to admit having made a mistake, and this was aggravated by his admission next morning: 'Had a feeling of disgust at having confessed to L. last night my fault.'

If one reflects that a very learned Dominican, for example, thinks nothing of prostrating himself on the floor in church in full view not only of his community, but if so happens also of a congregation, because he is a few minutes late for Mass or Office, it must certainly be admitted that Newman made rather heavy weather of confessing a slight fault to a fellow priest. But then we must remember not only that he had never had any training as a religious, but also that his position had been of such prominence, that he had been so unquestioningly accepted and looked up to as the leader of a most influential Movement, that the admission of some petty little fault must have cost him a good deal. It shows his determination to uproot this weakness that he resolved during his meditation 'to confess for a time the result of a particular examen on selfcomplacency to D.L. or Bowles, if no other way will do to repress the sin'. He further prayed 'against my present great aversion to the very name of penance'—a curious admission, seeing that so many of his sermons deal with this particular subject. But it is one thing to preach, quite another to do.

Of course, it has always been the habit of the saints to exaggerate their own sins and shortcomings; yet there is something very convincing in Newman's admission: 'I have only to observe that I seem unwilling to say, "Give me utter obscurity"; partly from a hankering after posthumous fame, partly from a dislike that others should do the work of God in the world and not I . . . I cannot bear contempt, when it comes in palpable instances.'

Again, these are the almost inevitable faults of the teacher and preacher, who has always exercised a great influence on others, of the ardent worker for God who knows only too well that no one else can do God's work as effectively as he. They are faults that are often hidden even from very good Christians. It was due to Newman's extraordinary clearsightedness that he recognized them in himself—but it needed many a 'dark night', to use the term of St John of the Cross, to rid him of these very natural imperfections, which might scarcely be considered faults in others, but which in those meant to be saints have to be purged. Newman himself was aware of this responsibility of his, for, as he writes in the same Retreat notes: 'There are persons, who, being destined by Providence to a high path, have no medium between it and hell; so that, if I do not pursue the former, I may be falling into the latter.'

After his Lenten Retreat he felt his position in the Church of England to have become increasingly precarious. As early as February 1843 he had publicly withdrawn his most violently anti-Catholic statements in a letter published in the *Conservative Journal*. In May Pusey preached a sermon on the Eucharist which was considered too 'Catholic' by the authorities who suspended him from preaching for two years. On August 23 Newman wrote to his friend E. L. Badely about it: 'Here is a solemn University Act in condemnation of a sermon, which is an understatement of a doctrine which must be called Catholic. . . . No acts at this time of the day surely can unchurch us, if we have not been unchurched by the events of the Reformation—but they may bring out, they may force on the mind, the fact we are, that we long have been unchurched.'

Only two days later he received a decisive personal shock:
William Lockhart, one of his young disciples who lived with him
at Littlemore and from whom he had exacted a promise not to
leave the Church of England for three years, had gone to Lough-
borough, where he met Father Gentili, a Rosminian* priest, and
after making a three days' retreat was about to be received into the
Catholic Church. 'This occurrence,' Newman wrote to his sister
Jemima, 'will very likely fix the time of my resigning St Mary's,
for he has been teaching in our school till he went away.' His
sister was greatly upset and answered by return of post. 'There are
so many anxious minds' she wrote, 'waiting and watching your
every motion, who would . . . consider it a beginning of a formal
disengaging of yourself from your own Church'. But she continues, and this shows the profound trust and veneration his own
family had for him: 'If the matter is settled in your mind, and
must be so, I trust the sense of having done what you thought
right will be your reward and my great consolation; for what
would become of me if I could not think of you, as I always have
thought with joy and gratitude, that I am your sister? Yes, dear
John, I feel it cannot be otherwise; whichever way you decide it
will be a noble and true part. . . .'

The anxiety his decision caused was not confined to his inti-
mates. A lady wrote to his sister at the same time, and her letter is
evidence of the tremendous spiritual influence he exercised in the
Church of England. She wrote in the name of all those 'who have
been used to look up to him as a guide. These people have a claim
upon him: he has witnessed to the world, and they have received
his witness; he has taught, and they have striven to be obedient
pupils. He has formed their minds, not accidentally: he has
sought to do so, and he has succeeded. . . . A sound from Littlemore and St Mary's seems to reach us even here, and has given
comfort on many a dreary day, but when that voice ceases, even
the words it has already spoken will lose some of their power; we
shall have sad thoughts as we read them.'

Jemima enclosed this letter in hers. Newman, too, replied by

* A congregation of priests founded by A. Rosmini in 1828.

return of post, telling her that these letters 'would have brought me to many tears unless I had so hard a heart. You must take what I do in faith . . . my circumstances are not of my making. One's duty is to act *under* circumstances. Is it a light thing to give up Littlemore? Am I not providing dreariness for myself? If others, whom I am pierced to think about, because I cannot help them, suffer, shall not I suffer in my own way?' And on the very next day, September 1, he wrote in a letter to his brother-in-law, James Mozley, marked 'Confidential': 'The truth then is, I am not a good son enough of the Church of England to feel I can in conscience hold preferment under her. I love the Church of Rome too well.'

And so, on September 18, 1843, he resigned St Mary's before a notary, and a week later he preached for the last time at Littlemore, the famous sermon on 'The Parting of Friends'. It is a most moving document, and it is not surprising that many of his audience should have been in tears at the end. He begins with the picture of Jesus eating the Passover with his disciples before his Passion, and it seems that the anguish Newman himself had undergone had given him a deeper understanding for the true humanity of the Incarnate Son. He is no longer afraid of attributing human feelings to him, for he can now write: 'He calls his friends around Him. . . . He bids them stay by Him, and see Him suffer; He desires their sympathy; He takes refuge in their love.' This is the suffering Christ on whom the Church meditates in Passiontide, whose human anguish has been the inspiration and the consolation of all its saints. Newman is no longer kept away from him by exaggerated reverence; his fasts and meditations at Littlemore have had their effect: he has penetrated more deeply into the mystery of the Cross.

His own feelings break out when he says of Jacob, who had to flee from Esau's wrath: 'He parted with all that his heart loved, and turned his face towards a strange land.' For Newman loved Oxford, he loved his friends, his work, his preaching and teaching in the familiar atmosphere of the Church of England and of the University in which he had been reared. He had wanted to give back to this Church the Catholic heritage he had been convinced was hers by right, but she had rejected him. And so at the end of the sermon he addresses her in a heartbreaking lament that sums up the suffering of many years: 'O my mother, whence is this unto thee, that thou hast good things poured upon thee and canst not keep them, and bearest children, yet darest not own them? Why hast thou not the skill to use their services, nor the heart to rejoice in their love? How is it that whatever is generous in purpose, and tender or deep in devotion, thy flower and thy promise, falls from thy bosom and finds no home in thine arms? . . . Thine own offspring, the fruit of thy womb, who love thee and would toil for thee, thou dost gaze upon with fear, as though a portent, or thou dost loathe as an offence—at best thou dost but endure, as if they had no claim on thy patience . . . to be rid of them as easily as thou mayest . . . or thou biddest them be gone, where they will be more welcome.'

Then he addresses his congregation, all those friends who had come to hear him preach for the last time: 'O my brethren, O kind and affectionate hearts, O loving friends, should you know any one whose lot it has been, by writing or by word of mouth, in some degree to help you thus [i.e. according to Christian principles] to act; if he has ever told you what you knew about yourselves, or what you did not know . . . if what he has said or done has ever made you take interest in him, and feel well inclined towards him; remember such a one in time to come, though you hear him not, and pray for him, that in all things he may know God's will, and at all times he may be ready to fulfil it.'

Newman descended from the pulpit, never again to preach in the Church of England. One who had attended his sermons speaks of 'the aching blank, the awful pause which fell on Oxford when that voice had ceased, and we knew that we should hear it no more. It was as when, to one kneeling by night, in the silence of some vast cathedral, the great bell tolling solemnly overhead has suddenly gone still. . . . Since then many voices of powerful teachers may have been heard, but none that ever penetrated the soul like his.'

G

But that Newman had given up St Mary's did not mean that he was straightway going to join the Church of Rome, though he felt irresistibly drawn to her. For he was still, as he wrote to his sister Harriet a few days later, 'in a state of doubt, of misgivings, of being unequal to responsibilities. . . . All I know is, that I could not without hypocrisy profess myself any longer a *teacher* and a *champion* for our Church.'

The next two years were spent at Littlemore in complete retirement, in prayer and study. Even his social life was severely curtailed, because, as he wrote to one of his friends: 'I am not worthy of friends. With my opinions, to the full of which I dare not confess, I feel like a guilty person with others, though I trust I am not so.' At the end of 1844 he determined to clarify his own thought by writing his *Essay on the Development of Christian Doctrine*, and then resolved (see *Apologia*) that if at the end of it his convictions about the Roman Church were not weaker, he would take the necessary steps for admission.

The Essay on Doctrinal Development is an extremely important work that has had an enormous influence on modern Catholic theology. It is not within the scope of this book to give even a bare résumé of it. There are, however, certain passages that are important for the evolution of Newman's spiritual teaching. First of all, his outlook had undergone a considerable change; he regarded Christianity no longer as so other-worldly as he had done before. In the Introduction to the Essay he writes: 'Its home is in the world; and to know what it is, we must seek it in the world, and hear the world's witness of it.' The somewhat one-sidedly moralistic outlook of the earlier years has gone; Newman now regards 'the Incarnation [as] the central aspect of Christianity', and from this follows that it has three main aspects, 'the sacramental, the hierarchical, and the ascetic. But one aspect of Revelation must not be allowed to exclude or to obscure the other; and Christianity is dogmatical, devotional, practical all at once . . . it is indulgent and strict; it is light and dark; it is love, and it is fear.'

Before, Newman had emphasized 'strictness' almost to the exclusion of indulgence; he had dwelt on the negative aspects of

Christianity, that is to say the horror of sin and the difficulty of leading a truly Christian life. But now he was approaching the Church that held out pardon to sinners as well as the ideal of Christian perfection realized in a host of saints of the most diverse character and achievements. 'They,' Newman writes, 'become instinct with His life, of one body with His flesh, divine sons, immortal kings, gods. He is in them, because He is in Human nature; and He communicates to them that nature, deified by becoming His, that them It may deify. He is in them by the Presence of His Spirit, and in them is He seen. They have those titles of honour by participation, which are properly His. Without misgiving we may apply to them the most sacred language of Psalmists and Prophets.' He is no longer afraid that this might be 'irreverent'. The saints of the Catholic Church have conquered his pessimism about human nature; for in Christ this human nature is raised to divine standards.

Now Newman gives a far larger place to the power of grace which, he says, 'is not only holy but sanctifying'. True, this 'cannot elevate and change us without mortifying our lower nature', but 'by the fact of an Incarnation we are taught that matter is an essential part of us, and, as well as mind, is *capable of sanctification*'. This means that Newman's spirituality is now becoming integrated with the whole of human life; he no longer holds, as he did in his earlier sermons, that 'Christianity . . . has ever been a restraint on the world rather than a guide to personal virtue and perfection on a large scale.' The annals of the saints have taught him otherwise. They have also taught him that love is the centre of the spiritual life rather than fear—which he had stressed earlier because he felt that in the Church of England of his time the Christian idea of love had been abused so as to condone sin. Now he writes: 'We know that no temper of mind is acceptable in the divine Presence without love; it is love which makes Christian fear differ from servile dread . . . yet in the beginning of the religious life, fear is the prominent evangelical grace, and love is but latent in fear, and has in course of time to be developed out of what seems its contradictory. Then, when it is developed, it

takes that prominent place which fear held before, yet protecting
not superseding it. Love is added, not fear removed, and the
mind is but perfected in grace by what seems a revolution.'

Once Newman had meant by 'mysticism' 'a neglect of Church
ordinances as such—and thinking to gain grace quite as well from
private devotion'. Now he realized that 'the highest devotion in
the Church is the mystical, and contemplation has been the token
of the most singularly favoured Saints'. For he had found what
he calls the 'Blessed Vision of Peace', the Church which proclaimed its power to forgive post-baptismal sin, of which he had
taken such a severe view in his *Parochial and Plain Sermon*, as well
as its power to sanctify both sinners and those who had never been
estranged from God.

For years Oxford, and indeed all England, had waited anxiously
for what would happen to the recluse at Littlemore. On October
6, 1845, he signed the 'Advertisement' to the *Essay on Development*. Two days later he wrote to his sister Jemima: 'I must tell
you, what will pain you greatly, but I will make it as short as you
would wish me to do. This night Father Dominic the Passionist,
sleeps here. He does not know of my intention, but I shall ask him
to receive me into what I believe to be the One Fold of the
Redeemer.'

The long struggle was over. The most influential son of the
Church of England in the nineteenth century had left her to find
peace in the Church of Rome.

5 'SPIRITUAL HONEYMOON'

I T was with a heavy heart that Newman made up his mind, after some hesitation, to leave Littlemore and Oxford, his spiritual as well as his physical home for almost thirty years. He left behind in the Church of England Keble and Pusey, his dear friends who had fought so many battles with him, and a whole host of associations, but he took with him some younger men who had looked up to him as their leader for a long time.

Newman's first reaction after the long struggle in Littlemore seems to have been exhaustion, for he wrote two months after his reception that all the converts 'but one' were full of peace and joy; but this did not affect his profound conviction of the truth of Catholicism. Indeed, he was 'now so convinced of the truth and divinity of the Catholic Church' that he writes to an inquirer in December 1835, 'I am pained about persons who are external to it in a way in which I was not before', and he who had tried to keep his friends within the Church of England even a few months before his conversion, was now most anxious that they should follow him into the Church of Rome, of which he had written twelve years ago that she did 'soothe the heart'.

After the first months of nervous exhaustion were over Newman threw himself with all his energy into his new life. He came to the Catholic Church as a learner; and he did what almost all sincere converts do in the first years after joining it: he suspended his critical faculties and accepted unquestioningly what it had to offer. At the end of February 1846 he left his beloved Littlemore looking back on the years he had spent there as the happiest time of his life, and fixed himself at Oscott near Birmingham, at a house he called Maryvale, given him by Bishop Wiseman with a view to forming a religious community. 'It is like going on the open sea,' he wrote to his younger friend Ambrose St John, who had preceded him into the Church by a few days and remained his faithful friend till death. In June he made his retreat before receiving Minor Orders. Meditating on the vocation of an apostle he wrote, significantly: 'I can say I am *willing* to follow Christ in poverty and reproach. I can say that "He would do with me whatever He will"—but I find it hard to pray that absolutely I may have poverty and reproach, since He had them, which is the third stage of humility. Without being able to analyse my feelings, I think I approached nearer to our Lord in this meditation than I am usually.'

This passage from his notes is very revealing in its honesty. It had become, and in many cases still is, a cliché of spiritual writers that truly 'spiritual' people must prefer poverty and reproach to the ordinary amenities of life. But for most, even very holy, people, this preference is something unreal. As Newman rightly says, one can willingly accept these when they come because such is God's will; it is something quite different actually to pray for them. Another note made during the same retreat shows that Newman's prayer became more and more simplified. He writes: 'I found I could go on meditating or rather dwelling on the *idea* itself of the Meditation without tiring—so much so that I did not know whether to go on from point to point—yet with very little thought or fruit—It being easy to dwell on the thought, I have no *effort* to make, and thus wandering thoughts came in and went out. The whole was rather passive than active.'

This simplified form of prayer without much actual thought and moving from one idea to another is the first stage of contemplation, when the mind is pacified and content to rest in the presence of God. Newman had experienced this already during his retreats at Littlemore, but it seems that he did not realize what it was, nor was he evidently encouraged to pursue this contemplative prayer, for he tried always to overcome what he called 'drowsiness', which is one of the signs that a man has passed the stage of intellectual meditation and is ready for the next. But he lived at a time when mysticism was deprecated even in the Catholic Church and the 'Exercises' of St Ignatius of Loyola were regarded as *the* standard form of mental prayer.

Shortly after this retreat he wrote to a friend, Mrs Lockhart, who was to be received into the Church in a few days: 'I will but add that the deep and awful joy which membership with the Catholic Church imparts is something different in kind from any peace I had in the Anglican . . . I am indeed too happy—and therefore I know it will not last—I shall have to go out into the world, and to be full of business and anxiety—and then I shall look back with kind and sad recollection at these days.' Nor were honours lacking. In March, Gregory XVI had sent him a silver Crucifix, and soon after his accession, the new Pope, Pius IX, sent him his blessing 'rather pointedly', as Newman says in a letter of August.

Newman's later description of this first year in the Church should therefore be taken with a grain of salt; for he wrote in his journal of 1863, when his reputation in the Church was at its lowest ebb: 'How dreary my first year at Maryvale . . . when I was the gaze of so many eyes at Oscott, as if some wild incomprehensible beast, caught by the hunter, and a spectacle for Dr Wiseman to exhibit to strangers, as himself being the hunter who captured it! I did not realize this at the time except its discomfort; but also, what I did realize, was the strangeness of ways, habits, religious observances, to which, however, I was urged on to conform without any delicacy towards my feelings . . . I was made an humiliation at my minor orders and at the examination for them; and I had to stand at Dr Wiseman's door waiting for Confession amid the Oscott boys. I did not realize these as indignities at the time, though, as I have said, I felt their dreariness.'

These are the exaggerations of a very disappointed man, as Newman was at that time; his letters written during his first year in the Church certainly tell a very different story. In January 1846, after having visited many Catholic priests and families he wrote: 'I was received with the most unaffected single-hearted kindness everywhere, and saw nothing but what made me feel admiration and awe of the system in which I find myself.' A few months later a friend wrote of him: 'As usual he is the life of the whole party, and keeps all cheerful and in good humour.' And in June, Newman himself told a friend: 'There is a grace in the Catholic Church which . . . binds the soul tight.'

Nor had he lost his sense of humour, for in September, when he and some friends had set out for Rome to study for the priesthood, he gives a very amusing description of French food and customs: 'Their mode of living is marvellous . . . we have had state breakfasts and dinners every day, consisting of a succession of dishes dressed in oil, the very number of which was enough to make one sick . . . the absurdest mockery of tea in tiny coffee cups. . . . And, to add to it, they are in utter astonishment that such fare disagrees with us. . . . At the same time their ceremony is most amusing—they have never done bowing in the most formal manner—St John has in vain asked how often we ought to bow on taking leave—and for me, who hardly ever made a formal bow in my life, I can hardly keep my countenance, as I put my elbows to my hips and make a segment of a circle, the lower vertebrae being the centre and my head the circumference.'

Such light-hearted chatter is hardly compatible with the picture of dreariness and humiliation Newman later gave in a moment of depression. Nor can it be said that he conformed to Catholic habits and observances against his will, for even two years later, in 1848, he wrote 'that every one who joins the Church, must come in the spirit of a child to a Mother—not to criticize any thing, but to accept' and about the same time he spoke enthusiastically of feeling oneself 'surrounded by all holy arms and defences—with the sacraments week by week . . . with crucifixes and rosaries which have been blessed, with holy water, with places or with acts to which Indulgences have been attached . . . what can one ask, what can one desire, more than this?' He also accepted unquestioningly the legends of the Holy House of Loreto, of the Blood of St Januarius and many other dubious stories and devotions, and in his 'Lectures on the Difficulties of Anglicanism' delivered in 1850 he promises his hearers that after they have joined the Church *now!*

'You will be so full of faith, that you will almost see invisible
mysteries, and will touch the threshold of eternity. And you will
be so full of joy that you will wish all round you to be partakers
of it, as if for your own relief.'

That the basic emotion in these years was joy not disappointment is further proved by *Loss and Gain*, a light-hearted conversion novel he wrote in 1847. Despite Newman the preacher's grave
warnings against novel-reading he himself had been an admirer
of Walter Scott, and later enjoyed particularly Thackeray and
Trollope. Now he wrote his own novel partly as an answer to an
absurd story *From Oxford to Rome* which had great success at the
time, though its author, one Miss Harris, was completely ignorant
of the Oxford converts, and partly to help a new Catholic pub-
lisher, 'poor Burns'. The book is an extraordinary mixture of exu-
berant gaiety and serious discussion. What could be funnier than
Mr Vincent's (one of the tutors) disquisition on the subject of tea:
'Put in a large quantity, pour on the water, turn off the liquor;
turn it off at once—don't let it stand; it becomes poisonous. I am
a great patron of tea; the poet truly says, "It cheers, but not
inebriates." It has sometimes a singular effect upon my nerves; it
makes me whistle—so people tell me; I am not conscious of it.
Sometimes, too, it has a dyspeptic effect. I find it does not do to
take it too hot; we English drink our liquors too hot. It is not a
French failing, no indeed. In France, that is the country, you get
nothing for breakfast but acid wine and grapes; this is the other
extreme, and has before now affected me awfully. Yet acids, too,
have a soothing, sedative effect upon one; lemonade especially.'
And he goes on to give advice about preventing flatulency, which
tea might sometimes produce, by adding 'a little camomile, not
a great deal', and warns against taking too much sugar with
it.

On the other hand, the novel is partly autobiographical, and
Newman's own spirituality comes frequently to the fore. Thus
when he describes the hero's constant awareness of God: 'Charles's
characteristic, perhaps above anything else, was an habitual sense
of the Divine Presence; a sense which, of course, did not insure

uninterrupted conformity of thought and deed to itself, but still there it was—the pillar of the cloud before him and guiding him. He felt himself to be God's creature, and responsible to Him—God's possession, not his own.'

This feeling of being led by God, of being responsible to him, of being in a special way under the divine Providence is indeed the guiding light of Newman's spiritual life, and the object of all his teaching, too, is to make men aware of the divine Presence by removing the obstacles to this awareness, sin and self-will. He feels that his own destiny, which 'he could not ultimately escape', was to become a Catholic, and therefore faith was given him not only to submit his judgement, but also his 'tastes and likeings, to the rule and usage of the Church'. And at the centre of this new life is the Mass: 'To me nothing is so consoling, so piercing, so thrilling, so overcoming, as the Mass. . . . It is not a mere form of words—it is a great action, the greatest action that can be on earth. It is, not the invocation merely, but, if I dare use the word, the evocation of the Eternal. He becomes present on the altar in flesh and blood, before whom angels bow and devils tremble. . . . There are little children there, and old men, and simple labourers, and students in seminaries . . . there are innocent maidens, and there are penitents; but out of these many minds rises one eucharist hymn, and the great Action is the measure and the scope of it.'

Compared with this tremendous experience of the eucharistic sacrifice, what could it matter to him that he disliked some of the fringe devotions of Catholics? He was absolutely certain that 'The Roman Catholic Church is the one only voice of God, the one only way of salvation'—compared with this nothing else mattered, not even the loss of friends, not even the loss of Oxford which he loved so much and of which he wrote in his novel: 'The spires and towers of the University came on his view, hallowed by how many tender associations. . . . There lay old Oxford before him, with its hills as gentle and its meadows as green as ever. At the first view of that beloved place, he stood still with folded arms, unable to proceed. . . . Whatever he was to gain by becoming a

Catholic, this he had lost; whatever he was to gain higher and better, at least this . . . he never could have again.' Oxford he had indeed lost, but he had gained something more precious than Oxford, which he described at the end of the novel: 'He was still kneeling in the church of the Passionists before the Tabernacle, in the possession of a deep peace and serenity of mind, which he had not thought possible on earth. It was more like the stillness which almost sensibly affects the ears, when a bell which had long been tolling stops, or when a vessel, after such tossing at sea, finds itself in harbour. It was such as to throw him back in memory on his earliest years, as if he were really beginning life again. . . . He went on kneeling, as if he were already in Heaven with the throne of God before him, and Angels around.'

Though this may not have been his experience immediately after his conversion, as he had written that all the converts 'but one' had been full of peace and joy, it reflected obviously his state of mind after he had overcome the exhaustion that had been an inevitable consequence of his long years of uncertainty. As we shall see later, all through his life as a Catholic he affirmed time and again that he had found perfect peace in the Church, whatever difficulties he might have with its earthly representatives. At the moment, however, these were still in the future.

Soon after his conversion it had become clear both to Newman and to Dr Wiseman that the 'Oxford converts', as he and his friends were called, should form some kind of community, and as early as February 1846 he told his fellow convert Frederic William Faber, who had also gathered some young men round him, that he was especially attracted to the Oratorians, the congregation which Wiseman had suggested. They were a congregation of priests founded by St Philip Neri who lived in community but without vows and owning property, dedicated particularly to the apostolate in the large cities. The Roman authorities approved the plan and by February 1847 his mind was made up. In April he made a Retreat prior to his ordination as a priest, the notes on which are very revealing of his state of mind. We must remember that he was forty-six at the time, a good twenty years older than

the normal age for ordination, a time when most men have lost
the first fervour of youth and appreciate the comforts of life much
more than in their twenties. Newman was no exception, and he
complained of his state in his Retreat notes: 'I have in my mind
a wound or cancer,' he wrote, 'the presence of which prevents me
from being a good Oratorian. . . . I am in the state of being able
to fulfil my duty conscientiously along a prescribed course, but I
cannot rise above it to a higher level. I creep along the ground, or
even run—well enough for one who creeps or runs, but I cannot
fly. I have not in me the elements required for rising or advancing.
So far as I know I do not desire anything of this world: I do not
desire riches, power or fame; but on the other hand I do not
like poverty, troubles, restrictions, inconveniences. Bad health I
fear as one does who has experienced it, and avoid bodily pain
more than I used to. I love the mean that lies between riches and
poverty, and that is a temptation for me; yet I hope that without
great difficulty I should be able to give up all that I have, if God
ordered it. I do not like a rule of life, although for eighteen years
I have wished to live a more or less regular life. I like tranquillity,
security, a life among friends, among books, untroubled by business cares—the life of an Epicurean in fact'—or, as might be said
less severely, the life of a scholar for which nature had fitted him,
such as had been lived, for example, though in the different
circumstances of the middle ages, by St Thomas Aquinas.

Newman then goes on to confess that 'the holiest customs of
the Church' embarrass him 'like a person acting in a new and unfamiliar role'—which is not surprising especially when we are told
what these customs were. The Mass, the Rosary, litanies, the Breviary gave him pleasure; what worried him was saying certain
prayers to gain indulgences and to make novenas (prayers said
during nine days for obtaining a certain grace); these, he says
'overwhelm my memory, are a weight on my mind, distract and
almost terrify me'. Precisely these are peripheral customs which
are very much played down in our own time; it is not surprising
that they should have been irksome to a man like Newman, occupied with the great doctrines of the Church and the urgent prob-

lems of contemporary Christianity. He then makes what may seem the astonishing admission that, whereas during his period at Littlemore he had gladly observed 'many things which are proper to Catholics—fasts, meditations, retreats, the use of the Breviary . . . now I undergo a reaction, as they say, and have not the courage to continue those things which I did willingly in the Anglican Church'.

Again, this is not really surprising; for all these practices were means of drawing him ever closer to the Catholic Church; when they had achieved this purpose they seemed far less attractive. Besides, his new manner of life, the difficulties of accustoming himself to new ways, the many cares of deciding on the establishment of a religious community made it impossible to continue the secluded life of Littlemore. Moreover, he felt acutely that he was no longer young, that his best years were spent; and it is no light thing for a man to begin anew in almost every way at the age of forty-six. He writes, indeed 'that subtle and delicate vigour of faith has become dulled in me', but these words have to be interpreted in conjunction with what has gone before: 'I have not lost either my intimate sense of the Divine Presence in every place, nor the good conscience and the peace of mind that flows therefrom.'

Newman never became familiar with the Catholic mystics, or he would have realized that what he had lost was not actually the 'vigour of faith' but the conscious feeling of it; that his faith, because it was not accompanied by his 'original confidence in God's boundless love for me' had not for this reason become 'dulled'. In fact, he was going through a long purification, in which his faith, far from being weakened, on the contrary was strengthened, while losing its emotional accompaniments. It was his preparation for the work he was destined to do for the Church —a work which seemed to have little success at the time, because his views were those of the twentieth rather than of the nineteenth century.

Having been ordained priest in Rome, Newman returned to Birmingham with a papal Brief empowering him to set up an

Oratory there, with such modifications of the original Oratorian Rule as were necessary to meet conditions in England. This was no easy task; especially as he was joined by Faber and his young men. They were a very emotional group, who threw themselves with reckless abandon into all that was most popular in Roman Catholicism and could not have enough of miracles and little devotions. It was hardly to be expected that the two groups of converts would get on together, and Newman had to use all his tact and forbearance to make life possible. Further, as all the members of the nascent Oratory were converts, and most of them highly individualistic Oxford men at that, they had never been broken in to the idea of religious obedience to a superior. Hence Newman, himself so recent a convert and quite unused to Roman procedures, had even more than the normal difficulties in setting up a new community. For example, Faber's young men, who were not even priests, had the impertinence to object to Newman's friendship with Ambrose St John whom they accused of influencing Newman against them, and Faber, instead of reprimanding them reported the fact to Newman, who actually had to defend his actions and ended his letter to Faber on the subject: 'I very much doubt, *much as I love both of them* [the two ringleaders of the opposition against him] whether we shall not love each other better at a little distance than very close, from what they have shown.' These difficulties led eventually to two Oratorian houses, one in Birmingham with Newman as superior, the other in London under Faber.

Newman as a superior could be severe when the occasion demanded it; he had to write to J. D. Dalgairns, who was later to give him a great deal of trouble: 'You have a great fault, which, if I put it harshly, I should call, contempt of others. . . . No one among us speaks against the old Catholic Priests, as you do; no one so laughs at the Bishop as you. . . . When you came here it was as if *you* were going to do *the* thing and others were "slow". All ways were slow but yours. You never asked my advice from the first in any thing.' Then he details the various occasions on which Dalgairns' behaviour upset the peace of the whole house, telling him that his safety 'lies in subjection; do not set up for yourself, wherever you are'.

But he had not only difficulties inside the community. Faber was publishing some saints' lives translated from the Italian and the French, full of all manner of marvels. These were attacked by the old Catholics, who were afraid of the impression they might make on Protestants. Though his own views on the matter were very different from Faber's, Newman had nevertheless to defend Faber as a member of his own community, and because the objections to the Saints' Lives were rather exaggerated—they could certainly not be called heretical, as one of their critics had suggested. Newman wrote to Faber personally, however, that he could not see 'that it is *possible* for the Oratory, against the wishes (if so) of Bishops and Clergy and laity, to begin a series of Italianisms . . . which cannot *literally* be defended, but must be explained as popular unscientific language'.

His own ideas about what saints' lives should be, ideas which are very important for his spirituality, are expressed in one of his *Historical Sketches*, the introductory chapter to St Chrysostom, though this was written several years after the controversy about the Saints' Lives. 'There are persons of warm imaginations,' Newman writes there, 'who can easily picture to themselves what they never saw. They can at will see Angels and Saints hovering over them when they are in church. . . . They can go home and draw what they have seen, from the vivid memory of what, while it lasted, was so transporting. I am not one of such; I am touched by my five senses, by what my eyes behold and my ears hear. I am touched by what I read about, not by what I myself create . . . I love St Paul more than one of those first Carmelites, his contemporaries [wholly legendary], whose names and acts no one ever heard of . . . what I want to trace and study is the real, hidden but human, life . . . and this I gain with difficulty from mere biographies. Those biographies are most valuable both as being true and as being edifying; they are true to the letter, as far as they record facts and acts . . . but actions are not enough for sanctity; we must have saintly motives; and as to these motives,

the actions themselves seldom carry the motives along with them.
In consequence, they are often supplied simply by the biographer
out of his own head. . . . The biographer in that case . . . has
become a commentator . . . I want to hear a Saint converse; I am
not content to look at him as a statue; his words are the index of
his hidden life . . . he is a man and a brother; he is one of ourselves. . . . Perhaps I shall be asked what I mean by "Life". I
mean a narrative which impresses the reader with the idea of
moral unity, identity, growth, continuity, personality. . . . Commonly, what is called "the Life", is little more than a collection
of anecdotes. . . . From such works I do but learn to pay devotion to an abstract and typical perfection under a certain particular
name; I do not know more of the real Saint who bore it than
before. . . . When I read St Augustine or St Basil [i.e. their own
writings], I hold converse with a beautiful grace-illuminated soul,
looking out into this world of sense, and leavening it with itself,
when I read a professed life of him, I am wandering in a labyrinth.' And Newman ends these observations with a remark which
is still very apposite: 'Here another great subject opens upon us
. . . I mean the endemic perennial fidget which possesses us
about giving scandal; facts are omitted in great histories, or glosses
put upon memorable acts, because they are thought not edifying,
whereas of all scandals such omissions, such glosses, are the
greatest.' (See Appendix.)

The recent case of the falsifications in St Teresa of Lisieux's
autobiography and in her photographs would certainly have scan-
dalized Newman. For him a saint was a human being with human
weaknesses as well as great virtues, not an insipid plaster image
surrounded by strings of virtues and miracles. Even today the
obsession with giving scandal is still topical, as is the obsession
with 'edification' as opposed to historical truth. Newman's own
essays on St John Chrysostom, Theodoret, St Benedict and others
are models of such an objective and very human presentation, for
he himself was, like Chrysostom whom he describes, 'a writer
who delights to ponder human nature and human affairs, to analyse the workings of the mind, and to contemplate what is sub-

jective to it'. This attitude is apparent also in his second (and last) novel *Callista*, begun in 1849 but not finished till 1856, the story of a young pagan girl artist of the third century, who is finally converted to Christianity and suffers martyrdom. Much of his own conversion experience is incorporated in this novel, and his intense devotion to Christ is expressed in the words he places on the lips of the priest Caecilius: 'There is but one Lover of souls, and He loves each one of us, as though there were no one else to love. He died for each one of us, as if there were no one else to die for. He died on the shameful cross. . . . The love which He inspires lasts, for it is the love of the Unchangeable. It satisfies, for He is inexhaustible. The nearer we draw to Him, the more triumphantly does He enter into us; the longer He dwells in us, the more intimately have we possession of Him. It is an espousal for eternity.'

Faber's ideas about hagiography, however, were very different from Newman's; he loved the Italian and Spanish ways of presenting a saint as a kind of compendium of super-human deeds and virtues without any individuality, and Newman wrote to a friend that he wished the life of St Rose (of Lima) had never been published, while yet loyally defending Faber against the exaggerated attacks on him.

In January 1849 Newman established the Oratory in Birmingham, and a few months later Faber and his men went to London. In Birmingham Newman preached a series of sermons attended by both Catholics and Protestants, which were published under the title of *Discourses to Mixed Congregations*.

The spirituality of these sermons differs considerably from that of his Oxford ones, especially as regards sin and sinners. While a member of the Church of England, Newman had held that the Church could not accommodate sinners and that even after repentance sin still left its mark. Now he teaches that 'our Lord, by His omnipotent grace, can make the soul [of the sinner] as clean as if it had never been unclean'. For the Sacrament of Penance, 'can undo the past. . . . No sinner, ever so odious, but may become a Saint'. His changed view of Christ, too, is becoming more

H

marked. Under the influence of Catholic teaching about the com-
passionate Heart of Jesus Newman's preaching increasingly lost
its excessive reverential fear; he could now write of Christ: 'He
took to Himself a man's heart that we might entrust our hearts
to Him', and he wrote a very rhetorical sermon on 'The Mental
Sufferings of our Lord in His Passion' which, however, sounds
more like an echo of Latin examples than authentic Newman.

Both love and grace play a larger part in these sermons than in
his Oxford ones. He says of the Magdalen that 'love was to her
. . . as a wound in the soul, so full of desire as to become anguish'
and that love alone secures the love of Christ and 'blots out sin'.

Though his awareness of the unseen world was as keen as ever,
he no longer subscribed to the poetic view that the world of nature
is ruled by angels. Now he speaks of 'a universe, material for the
most part and corruptible . . . huge globes, hurled into space,
and moving mechanically . . . next, life without sense, myriads
of trees and plants. . . . Millions of irrational creatures surround
us, and it would seem as though the Creator had left part of His
work in its original chaos . . .' and he draws the conclusion that
the world is full of mystery and that therefore it is not unreason-
able to believe in the mysteries of religion. His view of the world
has become far less romantic; at the same time he is less afraid
of the beauties of nature than in his Anglican days but looks at
them as 'the poorest and dimmest glimmerings of His glory'
which will teach men how infinitely more beautiful is their
Creator.

Newman had not, however, lost his capacity for stinging his
hearers into consciousness of being sinners; he still had frightening
words about the worldly man whose 'heart is the home of darkness, it has been handled, defiled, possessed by evil spirits; he is
a being without faith, and without hope' and about the poor man
who 'indulges his passions, thinks little of religion, puts off repentance' and who shall therefore 'be buried with Dives in hell'.

There is one passage in his sermon on 'Saintliness the Standard
of Christian Principle' which is so topical that I cannot refrain
from quoting it almost in full, for it castigates what he calls

'notoriety', or what we should perhaps call 'publicity'. 'Wealth is one idol of the day,' he tells his hearers, 'notoriety is a second. . . . Never could notoriety exist as it does now, in any former age of the world; now that the news of the hour from all parts of the world, private news as well as public, is brought day by day to every individual . . . hence notoriety, or the making a noise in the world, has come to be considered a great good in itself, and a ground of veneration. . . . Notoriety, or, as it may be called, newspaper fame, is to the many what style and fashion, to use the language of the world, are to those who are within the higher circles; it becomes to them a sort of idol worshipped for its own sake, and without any reference to the shape in which it comes before them. It may be an evil fame or a good fame; it may be the notoriety of a great statesman, or of a great preacher, or of a great speculator . . . or of a great criminal; of one who has laboured in the improvement of our schools, or hospitals, or prisons, or workhouses, or of one who has robbed his neighbour of his wife. It matters not; so that a man is talked much of, and read much of, he is thought much of; nay, let him even have died justly under the hands of the law, still he will be made a sort of martyr of . . . the question with men is, not whether he is great, or good, or wise, or holy; nor whether he is base, and vile, and odious, but whether he is in the mouths of men, whether he has centred on himself the attention of many . . . whether he has been (as it were) canonised in the publications of the hour.'

Thus Newman in 1849, when neither television 'personalities' nor film stars were even dreamt of. What he would have said of our 'pop culture' may easily be imagined. For Newman lived in the unseen world of the eternal verities which he tried to bring near to his hearers; but how could he do so if their imagination was filled with nothing but the fads of the moment? That is why he castigated mercilessly the sensationalism of his contemporaries; he knew that sensationalism is the enemy of religion because it feeds materialism and draws men away from the unseen world to what is most ephemeral and transitory.

In the first fervour of his Catholicism he was extremely hard on

Protestants—an attitude soon to be greatly mitigated. He accused them of having no faith but merely 'what looks like faith . . . a mere hereditary persuasion, not a personal principle'; indeed, he tells them that 'in spite of so much that is good in them, in spite of their sense of duty, their tenderness of conscience on many points, their benevolence . . . they are under the dominion (I must say it) of a proud fiend; they have this stout spirit with them, they determine to be their own masters in matters of thought'. But he is no less severe on Catholics, for he subscribes to the opinion that 'the number of Catholics that are to be saved will on the whole be small' and that 'Multitudes of those who never knew the Gospel will rise up in the judgement against the children of the Church, and will be shown to have done more with scantier opportunities'.

In 1850 he delivered lectures on *Certain Difficulties Felt by Anglicans in Catholic Teaching*, which shows a further development of his spirituality. Though he was still rather pessimistic and held that the Church represses evil rather than creates good, his views of sin and sinners were greatly influenced not only by the current moral text books but also by the practice of the confessional. He deprecates the virtues held most dear by what he calls 'the world'—'honesty, fairness, honour, truth, and benevolence—all of which', he admits, 'the teaching of the Church comprehends, all of which she expects in their degree in all her consistent children, and all of which she enacts in their fulness in her saints; but which, after all, most beautiful as they are, admit of being the fruit of nature as well as of grace; which do not necessarily imply grace at all' because they do not unite the soul to God. 'Take,' he says, 'a mere beggar-woman, lazy, ragged, and filthy, and not over-scrupulous of truth—(I do not say she had arrived at perfection)—but if she is chaste, and sober, and cheerful, and goes to her religious duties (and I am supposing not at all an impossible case), she will in the eyes of the Church, have a prospect of heaven, which is quite closed and refused to the State's pattern-man, the just, the upright, the generous, the honourable, the conscientious, if he be all this, not from a supernatural power

—(I do not determine whether this likely to be the fact, but I am contrasting views and principles)—not from a supernatural power, but from mere natural virtue.'

The saving qualification in this sweeping statement is, of course, the last sentence in brackets. For it does, indeed, seem improbable that such an ideal 'State's pattern-man' could exist without the concourse of grace, and that such a man would be debarred from heaven. But what Newman wants to emphasize here is that non-respectable but devout Christians may be more loved by God than the highly respectable and respected members of society—a view that is certainly borne out by the New Testament, which shows Christ consorting with harlots and tax collectors. For Newman the Catholic priest now realizes what the fellow of Oriel and vicar of St Mary's did not, namely that the Church is not only the Church of 'consistent Christians', but also the Church of sinners who need forgiveness again and again. For, he says in the same sermon on 'The Social State of Catholic Countries no Prejudice to the Sanctity of the Church' from which I have just quoted, the Church 'cannot disguise from herself, that, with whatever advantages her children commence their course, in spite of their baptism, in spite of their most careful education and training, still the great multitude of them require her present and continual succour to keep them or rescue them from a state of mortal sin'.

He is, however, by no means blind to the defects of Catholicism on its human side and admits that 'the restless mind of a Protestant, who sets the Divine Will before him . . . and wishes to be taught and wishes to believe, may have more of grace in it, and be more acceptable in the divine sight, than his, who only believes passively'. For such a passive state of mind will resist all change which, as he had shown in his *Essay on Development*, is of the very essence of life. He therefore writes that 'the faultiness of this passive state of mind is detected, whenever a new definition of doctrine is promulgated. . . . Its immediate tendency, as exhibited in a population, will be to resist it, simply because it is new . . . whereas a ready and easy acceptance of the apparent novelty

. . . may be the very evidence of a mind, which has lived, not merely in certain doctrines, but in those doctrines as revealed—not simply in a Creed, but in its Giver—or, in other words, which has lived by real faith.'

We have seen this tendency to resist all change in our own time in the reluctance to accept the new Liturgy and other measures promulgated by the Second Vatican Council, even though these were not new dogmas. Newman himself once thought that change should be resisted, when he wanted to build his faith exclusively on the teaching of the early Fathers of the Church and considered the additions made in the Catholic Church as deformations of the ancient faith, until he realized that these additions were not signs of decadence but of life. Indeed he accepted changes in the ritual as a matter of course, as is clear from one of his letters written at the same time with reference to the neo-Gothic churches of Pugin which he disliked intensely: 'Now if the rites of the Church have *changed*, let the architecture *develop*—let it modify and improve itself to meet them. No, says Mr Pugin. . . .'

This openness to change in all departments of the life of the Church makes Newman's spirituality extremely modern. Because of his humility, however, he did not realize that he himself also embodied a new form of sanctity when he anxiously rejected the idea of his own holiness in a letter to Miss Munro, a convert whose spiritual director he was.

'I have nothing of a Saint about me,' he writes, 'as everyone knows, and it is a severe (and salutary) mortification to be thought next door to one. I may have a high view of many things, but it is the consequence of education and of a peculiar cast of intellect —but this is very different from *being* what I admire. I have no tendency to be a saint—it is a sad thing to say. Saints are not literary men, they do not love the classics, they do not write Tales. I may be well enough in my way, but it is not the "high line". People ought to feel this, most people do. But those who are at a distance have fee-fo-fum notions about one. It is enough for me to black the saints' shoes—if St Philip uses blacking, in heaven.'

Eighteen hundred and fifty-one was a crucial year for Newman,

for it initiated the long period of suffering for and through the
Church in which his spirituality reached its maturity. It was
marked by three events: his lectures on the *Present Position of
Catholics in England*, occasioned by the violent reactions to the
restoration of the Catholic hierarchy in England which until then
had been treated as a 'missionary' country; the beginning of the
Achilli trial that resulted from these lectures and Newman's
appointment as rector of the Catholic University which was to be
established in Ireland.

In his lectures Newman defended his Church with all the ora-
torical powers at his disposal: brilliant irony and wit, logic and
a tremendous store of knowledge combined to produce a shatter-
ing indictment of the ingrained Protestant prejudice of nineteenth-
century England against Catholicism and a glowing vindication
of Catholic doctrine and practices. He showed that belief in
miracles and the power of relics are but consequences of the Incarnation, in which Protestants also believed, and he violently
attacked the absurd tales about Catholics circulated in such books
as 'Maria Monk' and the writings of Dr Giovanni Achilli about
the Inquisition.

Achilli was an ex-Dominican friar who had been unfrocked for
immorality and who was taken up by a Protestant association in
England where he lectured on the supposed iniquities of the
Catholic authorities. Cardinal Wiseman had exposed him in the
Dublin Review the year before and his article had produced no
controversy. Before repeating Wiseman's statements in his lectures
Newman consulted his legal advisers who told him that there
would be little danger of a libel action, especially as there was
abundant proof of the truth of the accusations. So Newman went
ahead, confident that no ill could come of repeating in his lectures
what had gone unnoticed in the *Dublin Review*.

In the uproar that was to follow Newman's denunciation of
Achilli, and which was to hold Catholics not only in England but
throughout the world in suspense for the next two years, some
very remarkable observations in the last of these lectures went
almost unnoticed. They concerned Newman's views of the posi-

tion of the laity in the Church, views which are as important for
his spirituality as they were for his later sufferings at the hands
of the Roman authorities.

For him laymen were not a kind of second-rate Christians, and
their spirituality was not to consist in some childish repetition
of pious tales. 'What I desiderate in Catholics,' he wrote, 'is the
gift of bringing out what their religion is. . . . I want a laity,
not arrogant, not rash in speech, not disputatious, but men who
know their religion, who enter it, who know just where they
stand, who know what they hold, and what they do not, who
know their creed so well, that they can give an account of it, who
know so much of history that they can defend it. I want an intelligent, well-instructed laity. . . . I wish you to enlarge your knowledge, to cultivate your reason, to get an insight into the relation
of truth to truth, to learn to view things as they are, to understand
how faith and reason stand to each other, what are the basis and
principles of Catholicism. . . . I have no apprehension you will
be the worse Catholics for familiarity with these subjects, provided
you cherish a vivid sense of God above, and keep in mind that you
have souls to be judged and to be saved.' And he goes on to say
that 'Cultivation of mind . . . is not the same thing as religious
principle, but it contributes much to remove from our path the
temptation to many lesser forms of moral obliquity. Human
nature, left to itself, is susceptible of innumerable feelings, more or
less unbecoming, indecorous, petty, and miserable. . . . Mental
cultivation, though it does not of itself touch the greater wounds
of human nature, does a good deal for these lesser defects.'

These were revolutionary words in his time—just how revolutionary will be seen later. They show also a considerable difference
from what he had said about twenty years before in his Anglican
sermons. Then he had spoken to highly educated men whom he
had to warn against the dangers of mere intellectual enjoyment.
Now he was confronting rather simple-minded Catholics who
had been used to leaving the solution of most of their religious
and moral problems to their priests, whose spirituality was not
supported by intellectual knowledge of their religion, and who

could not give an account of their religion if challenged. The idea
that the laity should be able to meet the Protestant challenge, that
they should not be content with an external performance of their
duties but that they should penetrate more deeply into the mysteries of their religion was almost unheard-of. In his letters of this
period Newman constantly urged a greater influence for the laity;
he complained that laymen were never consulted on the subject
of the restoration of the hierarchy, and he was sorry that his own
bishop, W. B. Ullathorne, 'has a horror of laymen', whereas Newman himself was 'sure they may be made in this day the strength
of the Church'. In fact, immediately after Newman had delivered
this last of his lectures, Ullathorne wrote to him on September 3
expressing his fear that such teaching might encourage 'the poorer
classes especially the Irish' in their 'love of religious controversy'.

But these misgivings were overshadowed by the great trial that
was now coming upon him, and which he seems to have anticipated when he wrote, in the same last lecture: 'For myself, I confess I have no love of suffering at all; nor am I at a time of life
when a man commonly loves to risk it. To be quiet and to be
undisturbed, to be at peace with all, to live in the sight of my
brethren, to meditate on the future and to die—such is the prospect, which is rather suitable to such as me. Yet, my Brothers, I
have no doubt at all, either about myself or about Catholics generally, if trial came. I doubt not we should suffer any trial well, not
from nature, but from grace; not from what we are in ourselves,
but from the wonder-working power which is amongst us, and
which fills us as vessels, according to our various dimensions.'

These were prophetic words; for they mark the end of the
'honeymoon' period. Newman, the brilliant convert from Oxford,
had been received with open arms into the Church whose most
influential representatives were so very different from him, the
least 'clerical' of men. But before the difference became obvious
there was a brief period during which, whatever his personal
sufferings, he was acclaimed as the representative of English
Catholicism—the period of the Achilli trial.

6 INTELLECT AND SPIRITUALITY

NEWMAN might have been spared a long period of anxiety, if Wiseman had supplied the material on which his accusations against Achilli in the *Dublin Review* had been based. But he disregarded Newman's repeated requests for this material, which would have exonerated him from the accusation of 'libel' and prevented a trial, until it was too late, when, as Newman says in a letter 'he [Wiseman] looked [for it] and immediately found'. It was the first instance of episcopal procrastination from which he was to suffer so much in the years to come. For by the time Wiseman had sent the necessary papers, Achilli had initiated a criminal libel action and Newman had to produce witnesses for the acts of immorality of which, trusting the authority of Wiseman's article, he had accused Achilli.

The Achilli trial dragged on for about fifteen months, during which Newman had to send out his friends to Italy and Malta to persuade the women with whom the ex-Dominican had had immoral relations to come to England and witness in court. Both judge and jury were militant Protestants violently prejudiced against anything Catholic.

Newman's letters and diaries of this anxious time bear testimony to his deep and at the same time very human spirituality. From the first he regarded the trial as an attack of the demonic powers upon the Church: 'Achilli is going about like a false spirit' he wrote to George Talbot, then an influential canon of St Peter's in Rome, 'telling lies, and since it is forced upon us, we must put him down, and not suffer him to triumph', and a few months later to a nun: 'Since the middle of August I have been saying

with St Andrew, *O bona Crux, diu desiderata.**. . . I have anticipated evil from the first—i.e. if it can be called evil—anyhow
it is no harm to offer myself in expectation and in will, a sacrifice
to Him who bore the judgement seat and the prison of the un-
believer. When it flashed on my mind in the beginning of September that I might go to prison, I said: "May I come out a
Saint!" I don't say that now when things are more real, but "May
I be accepted for my Sins". I have all my life been speaking about
suffering for the Truth—now it has come upon me.'

There was a very real danger of his going to prison, a much
more fearful prospect for a man like him in Victorian England
than to us whose susceptibilities are perhaps blunted by the horrors
of our own time, the unspeakable sufferings of men, women and
children in Nazi concentration camps and hard labour in Siberia.
But for a fastidious scholar like Newman a year in prison, which
was then regarded by his legal advisers as a distinct probability,
in the squalor and the company of common criminals which this
inevitably entailed, a year in such conditions would have been a
true martyrdom that might easily have cost his life or at least
his health.

'It is strange that a matter, which, had I the little finger of a
saint in me, I should think nothing of, should so try me,' he writes
in a letter to his fellow Oratorian Dalgairns. But a long drawn
out trial with the prospect of a prison term at the end is no easy
matter in the best of circumstances, and what aggravated it in
Newman's case was that he had all his ordinary work to do and
moreover, was supposed to found a Catholic University in Ireland
just then and had to write lectures in preparation for it. One need
only read the enormous correspondence of this time, the endless
letters to legal advisers, the instructions to his friends for entertain-
ing the witnesses and shielding them from bribery, which Achilli's
supporters were sure to attempt, to realize how much all these
cares preyed on his mind and hindered his work.

Yet he remained convinced that all his sufferings were 'only for

---

* Words attributed to the apostle during his martyrdom in the Roman Breviary:
O good Cross, long desired.

some greater good'. His strong conviction of being led by God, which had been with him all through his life, did not desert him now. 'I have no misgivings,' he wrote in another letter to an Oratorian, 'I cannot wish it otherwise. It is God's hand; it is His purpose.' Therefore one 'must cultivate a lightness of heart . . . deeply based on faith'. He was certain that spiritual help alone could carry him through and asked the prayers of all the nuns he knew, being convinced that 'nothing but the intercession of the Blessed Virgin kept me up to my work'.

The 'lightness of heart' which he enjoined came out quite often in humorous asides in his correspondence; so, after asking the nuns' prayers he told them: '. . . if I failed, I should say "It's all those idle nuns", so, if I succeed, thro' God's mercy, I shall say "It's all those good, zealous persevering nuns".' And when his friends found it difficult to keep the witnesses, especially the husband of one of them, amused while waiting for the trial to begin he wrote: 'We think you don't allow Gippina's husband cigars enough—let him have an unlimited supply. Let him have anything else he takes to . . . is there no equestrial exhibition? no harmless play? No giant or dwarf? No panorama, cosmorama, diorama, dissolving views, steam incubation of chickens, or *menagerie* which he would like to see. Surely beasts are just the thing for him' while just before the beginning of the trial he joked: 'I am to be had up next Monday, and have two or three medical affidavits to the effect that imprisonment has a fair chance of killing me—but perhaps Johnny Campbell [the Lord Chief Justice] may wish to be Jack the Giant killer.'

Newman's own attitude during the trial made a deep impression on those who knew him. 'His time was spent day and night almost, before the Tabernacle, and his serenity and calmness in the midst of the excitement without were remarkable.'

He finally received a nominal sentence, being fined one hundred pounds, which was paid on the spot. (Catholics all over the world had collected such a large sum for the expenses of the trial that a few thousand pounds were left over and used by Newman for various charitable purposes.)

The Judge, Sir John Taylor Coleridge, a former friend of Newman, however, considered it a good opportunity to lecture him
on the deterioration of his character after he had become a Catholic
and finally begged him never again to engage in controversy except 'in a spirit of charity and of humility'. Nevertheless, he had
misgivings afterwards and wrote in his diary of January 31, 1853:
'Newman appeared today to receive his sentence. I did my part
but lamely. . . . But I was overpowered. The immense crowd,
the anxious and critical audience, his slender figure, and strange
mysterious cloudy face. After all the speeches of Counsel he desired
to say a few words, Oh! What a sweet musical, almost unearthly
voice it was, so unlike any other we had heard . . . I have a
feeling that there was something almost out of place in my not
merely pronouncing sentence on him, but in a way lecturing
him. . . .'

There can scarcely be a more convincing evidence to Newman's
tremendous spiritual personality than this admission from a very
unwilling witness. In the end he was not allowed to speak, but
the nominal sentence imposed on him because he could not prove
all the incidents he had mentioned in his Lectures was sufficient
evidence that he had gained a great moral, if not a legal, victory.

All through the agonizing time of the Achilli affair Newman
was occupied with a project for which he was uniquely qualified,
but which foundered in the end for a variety of reasons, especially
for lack of episcopal co-operation and of a sufficiently interested
laity. This project was the establishment of a Catholic University
in Dublin. It was a project that involved Newman in a multitude
of petty activities which he enumerates in a letter to Henry Wilberforce: 'My letters are a daily burden. . . . Every hour or half
hour of the day I have people calling on me. I have to entertain
strangers at dinner, I have to attend inaugural Lectures—four last
week, I have to stop Professors resigning, and Houses revolting.
I have to keep accounts and find money, when I have none. Besides
the book I have just published at Longmans', I have three reprint-
ing which I am reading thro' and correcting; and I have to pro-
vide four Sermons in print by St Paul's day, that for Sunday week

not having the first word written yet. I have to Lecture on Latin Composition, and examine for Exhibitions. . . .'

It seems almost incredible that he had to do all this himself, being his own secretary and accountant, to say nothing of the absence of typewriters and tape recorders at that time. But despite all these demands on his time and energy, in all this hubbub he wrote one of his most important works, *The Idea of a University,* as well as a series of sermons which, though not actually dealing with spirituality as such, are nevertheless very important for the question of the relation between spirituality and intellectual culture. In Christian antiquity as well as in the golden age of scholasticism, the two had often been combined; Origen and Gregory of Nyssa, St Albert and St Thomas Aquinas were all highly educated men, well versed also in subjects not directly belonging to the Christian faith. But side by side with these there had also been those who considered any occupation with 'secular' subjects detrimental to the spiritual life; such were many of the Eastern monks, such were saints like St Bernard and St John of the Cross, who felt that true union with God could only be reached if all earthly interests were completely rejected. The increasing departmentalization of modern life helped this tendency enormously; spirituality became a branch of its own, whose representatives spoke about men almost exclusively as 'souls', taking them out of their daily life to situate them at their 'prie-dieu'.

The unquestioning faith of the 'Breton peasant' was only too often held up as an ideal to those who, not being Breton peasants, simply could not help asking questions and, receiving at best dusty answers, were only too easily tempted to leave the Church and Christianity altogether. Newman saw, as only very few Catholics did at that time, that the spiritual life could not be divorced from the intellectual life, indeed, that far from harming spiritual life, intellectual culture, if rightly used, was aiding it. In a spirit very different from that of his Anglican sermon on the 'Danger of Accomplishments' he now wrote that the first obvious advantage of the pursuit of knowledge is to draw 'the mind off from things which will harm it to subjects which are worthy of a rational being', for 'knowledge, the discipline by which it is gained, and the tastes which it forms, have a natural tendency to refine the mind, and to give it an indisposition, simply natural, yet real . . . towards excesses and enormities of evil, which are often or ordinarily reached at length by those who are not careful from the first to set themselves against what is vicious and criminal'. It is, as Newman says, 'a safeguard', the value of which can scarcely be exaggerated; for it is a form of asceticism and may thus well be compared to what the mystics call detachment, the first step in the spiritual life that withdraws a man from enslavement to the grosser pleasures of sense.

Newman is well aware, however, that this cultivation of the intellect, while removing temptations to fall into the grosser sins, also has its own dangers, for it gives 'accidental opportunity to religious error, rash speculation, doubt, and infidelity', and that 'where power of intellect is, there need not be virtue; and that where right, and goodness, and moral greatness are, there need not be talent'.

For Newman the object of a Catholic University is to marry the two: to give the intellect its necessary freedom while forming a character steeped in the faith and ready to fulfil its demands. He is well aware of the temptation to think that 'religious people are commonly either very dull or very tiresome, nay, that religion itself after all is more suitable to women and children, who live at home, than to men'. He does not say that this is necessarily due to lack of humility, but knows that the reason is only too often that religion is presented in a childish way, divorced from the intellect. He fully admits that 'Young men feel a consciousness of certain faculties within them, which demand exercise, aspirations which must have an object, for which they do not commonly find exercise or object in religious circles. This want is no excuse for them, if they think, say or do anything against faith or morals; but still it is the occasion of their sinning.' Therefore Newman wants universities 'to be at once oracles of philosophy and shrines of devotion. It will not satisfy me, what satisfies so many, to have two independent systems, intellectual and religious, going at once side by side, by a sort of division of labour. . . . It will not satisfy me, if religion is here, and science there . . . It is not touching the evil to which these remarks have been directed, if young men eat and drink and sleep in one place, and think in another : I want the same roof to contain both the intellectual and moral discipline. . . . I want the intellectual layman to be religious, and the devout ecclesiastic to be intellectual. . . . Youths need a masculine religion, if it is to carry captive their restless imaginations, and their wild intellects, as well as to touch their susceptible hearts.'

In one of his sermons preached before the University of Ireland Newman tells his hearers that there are two types of saints, some 'who are so absorbed in the divine life, that they seem, even while they are in the flesh, to have no part in earth or in human nature; but to think, speak, and act under views, affections, and motives simply supernatural'. But then there are others (and they are the ones he places before his hearers as their examples) 'in whom the supernatural combines with nature, instead of superseding it— invigorating it, elevating it, ennobling it; and who are not the less men, because they are saints. They do not put away their natural endowments, but use them to the glory of the Giver; they do not act beside them, but through them; they do not eclipse them by the brightness of divine grace, but only transfigure them. They are versed in human knowledge; they are busy in human society; they understand the human heart; they can throw themselves into the minds of other men; and all this is consequence of natural gifts and secular education. While they themselves stand secure in the blessedness of purity and peace, they can follow in imagination the ten thousand aberrations of pride, passion, and remorse. The world is to them a book, to which they are drawn for its own sake, which they read fluently, which interests them naturally—though, by the reason of the grace which dwells within them, they study it and hold converse with it for the glory of God and the salvation of souls.'

Even in our time the first kind of sanctity is sometimes held to be the only, or at least the superior one; saints like St Francis of Assisi and St Teresa of Lisieux, whose lives and interests were centred in

God alone and who were wholly indifferent to the pursuits of
'the world' are far more popular than St Thomas Aquinas or
St Robert Bellarmine. Now it is quite true that in our materialistic
age men and women like the former, too, are greatly needed;
religious like, for example, the American Trappist Thomas Merton, who leave all secular ambitions to demonstrate to the world
'the one thing necessary'. But the other type of sanctity, the one
that Newman advocated in the sermon from which we have just
quoted and throughout his *Idea of a University* is, perhaps, at
least as necessary today and possibly even more difficult to achieve.
For the pure contemplatives in their retreats have indeed a tremendous supernatural power, they may through their intercession
convert many sinners—but they cannot influence the climate of
opinion, they cannot help to solve the great intellectual problems
of the time, they cannot make Christianity more acceptable to
scholars and scientists.

Now Newman's object, both in his own work and in his idea of
a university was precisely this. He was not afraid that secular
interests might draw a man away from God if he was truly
grounded in his religion, if his religion was allowed to grow
together with his other interests. For he foresaw the growing
spread of unbelief, which he considered, indeed, 'unavoidable in
an age of intellect and in a world like this', and he was only too
well aware of the fascination of modern sciences owing to 'their
marvellous results'—even though these results were far less marvellous in 1852 than they are in our own age of space travel and
nuclear research. For this reason he demanded a special theological
education for laymen, for, he writes, 'It will not answer the purpose for a Catholic to say, "I leave it to theologians", "I will ask
my priest".' No, Newman 'would have students apply their minds
to such religious topics as laymen actually do treat', such as 'an
intelligent apprehension of the relations . . . between the Church
and Society at large; for instance, the difference between the
Church and a religious sect; the respective prerogatives of the
Church and the civil power; what the Church claims of necessity,
what it cannot dispense with, what it can; what it can grant, what

I

it cannot. A Catholic hears the celibacy of the clergy discussed
in general society; is that usage a matter of faith, or is it not of
faith? . . . Nor will argument itself be out of place in the hands
of laymen mixing with the world. . . . Theologians inculcate the
matter, and determine the details of that Revelation; they view it
from within; philosophers view it from without, and this external
view may be called the Philosophy of Religion, and the office of
delineating it externally is most gracefully performed by laymen.'

Lay influence is, of course, most evident in the relations between
'Christianity and Scientific Investigation'; the lecture on this subject was never delivered, because it was considered 'inexpedient',
and it does, indeed, contain ideas that are only just beginning to
be approved in our own time. For centuries many spiritual writers
and theologians had repeated that the material world is a mere
nothing, unworthy of the attention of a Christian; Newman
writes: 'There is but one thought greater than that of the universe,
and that is the thought of its Maker.' And because he was poign-
antly aware of the mysteries of the universe, the apparent infinity
of space and the riddle of time—in a way unknown to the
medieval theologians with their tidy world of a stationary earth
surrounded by sun, moon and stars—he stood in awe before the
Creator who, 'though One, is a sort of world of worlds in Himself,
giving birth in our minds to an indefinite number of distinct
truths, each ineffably more mysterious than any thing that is found
in this universe of space and time'.

Nevertheless, the science of the universe has its own rights. 'The
whole universe,' writes Newman, 'comes from the good God. It
is His creation; *it* is good; it is all good, as being the work of the
Good, though good only in its degree, and not after His Infinite
Perfection.' Therefore its investigation, too, is a proper human
activity, and ought not to be restricted. '. . . free discussion is,'
says Newman, 'simply necessary for progress in Science. . . . I
say, then, that it is a matter of primary importance in the cultivation of those sciences, in which truth is discoverable by the human
intellect, that the investigator should be free, independent, un-
shackled in his movements; that he should be allowed and enabled,

without impediment, to fix his mind intently, nay, exclusively, on his special object, without the risk of being distracted every other minute in the process of his inquiry, by charges of temerariousness, or by warnings against extravagance or scandal.'

These portentous words were written twelve years before the publication of the notorious *Syllabus Errorum* which, while rightly censuring much that was obviously hostile to the Christian faith, produced an atmosphere of suspicion and fear in the Church from which it is being gradually freed only in our own day. No wonder, then, that this lecture was considered 'inexpedient'. But Newman foresaw that, unless modern ideas were allowed to be freely discussed Christianity would continue to lose ground, for: 'Great minds need elbow-room, not indeed in the domain of faith, but of thought. And so indeed do lesser minds, and all minds.' Newman could allow this freedom because his own faith was so firm. 'I say, then, he who believes Revelation with that absolute faith which is the prerogative of a Catholic, is not the nervous creature who startles at every sudden sound, and is fluttered by every strange or novel appearance which meets his eyes. He has no sort of apprehension, he laughs at the idea, that anything can be discovered by any other scientific method, which can contradict any one of the dogmas of his religion. . . . He is sure . . . that, if anything seems to be proved by astronomer, or geologist, or chronologist, or antiquarian, or ethnologist, in contradiction to the dogmas of faith, that point will eventually turn out, first, *not* to be proved, or, secondly, not *contradictory*, or, thirdly, not contradictory to any thing *really revealed*, but to something which has been confused with revelation . . . he will commit the matter to reason, reflection, sober judgement, common sense; to Time, the great interpreter of so many secrets.'

At first glance these passages quoted at such length seem to have little to do with spirituality. But on further reflection they will be found to be quite fundamental to Newman's spiritual life and teaching. For these rest on his firm conviction of the unity of truth, whether spiritual, doctrinal, scientific, historical or whatever else. Truth is ever one and ever the same—but our understanding of it progresses. This is his idea of development; as doctrine develops, so does our understanding of it in the light of new discoveries. Revelation, indeed, is true and has been given once and for all, but our understanding of it has not always been fault-less. The creation story, for example, once taken literally as directly revealed, is now seen to be a poetic description, in two versions, of early Semitic ideas about the coming into being of the universe, while the nucleus, the fact that the universe is a divine creation, is a revealed truth.

As will be seen later when we consider his controversy with Pusey, Newman makes no distinction between 'truth' and 'devotion', he does not allow devotion to feed on conceptions that are known to be not true. The stress here is on 'known'. In earlier ages many things were accepted as true that today are known to be false. Newman himself still wrote 'the preservation of our race in Noah's ark is an historical fact, which history never would arrive at without Revelation; and in the province of physiology and moral philosophy, our race's progress and perfectibility is a dream, because Revelation contradicts it'—assertions which he would no doubt not have made if he had lived today, in view of the new methods of Biblical criticism and the evolutionary theories of Teilhard de Chardin and others. For, as he himself said : 'If we reason, we must submit to the conditions of reason. We cannot use it by halves; we must use it as proceeding from Him who has also given us Revelation; and to be ever interrupting its processes, and diverting its attention by objections brought from a higher know-ledge . . . argues surely some distrust either in the powers of Reason on the one hand, or the certainty of Revealed Truth on the other.' The surer we are of God's revelation, the more readily shall we accept the modifications that reason forces us to make in our understanding of it.

Newman's spirituality, then, is an adult spirituality that does not need emotional props. Indeed, in his sermon on 'University Preaching' he insists that the preacher should be 'addressing him-self to the intellect of men . . . convincing as well as persuading.' Furthermore, 'he should set out with the intention of conveying to others some spiritual benefit . . . he should select some distinct fact or scene, some passage in history, some truth, simple or profound, some doctrine, some principle, or some sentiment . . . thus he should employ himself . . . to bring home to others, and to leave deep within them, what he has, before he began to speak to them, brought home to himself'.

This modern, intellectual spirituality was, in fact, one of the basic reasons for the troubles that arose between the Birmingham Oratory, governed by Newman, and its daughter house in London, which was under the direction of Faber. The divergence between the two Oratories had already become obvious in the differing attitudes of Newman and Faber to the Lives of the Saints; their views of sanctity and of the spiritual life could not but clash. The Brompton House (in London) accepted with alacrity all sentimentalities and exaggerations of Italian devotion, which Newman considered quite suitable for Southern temperaments, but repugnant to the English character. The London Oratorians would call the Blessed Virgin their dear 'Mama' and use a host of 'little' devotions of all kinds; they were much opposed to intellectual activity which they considered unspiritual. The material cause of the clash which ended in the complete separation of the two Oratories was, characteristically, the point of their Rule which forbade Oratorians to undertake the direction of nuns and similar works which would take them away from their own houses. Now the direction of nuns was just what one member, J. D. Dalgairns, at that time of Newman's own house, and the London Oratorians with their 'mystical' leanings liked particularly, and so they applied straightway to the Roman authorities for a change in their Rule without so much as letting Newman know what they had done. Naturally Newman, as the Founder of the English Oratory, was indignant at such highhanded and secretive procedure, and the rift between the two houses that inevitably followed and the endless discussions caused him deep anxiety as well as personal suffering and disappointment.

There can be no doubt that the London House was far more flamboyant and externally successful than the modest and, as one of Newman's friends called it, 'masculine' mother-house at Birmingham. Faber made a number of converts of high social standing and wrote spiritual books that became very popular owing to their tremendously emotional tone, while Newman wrote lectures that could be appreciated only by the intellectual few and besides devoted himself to the businessmen and workers of Birmingham, who did not hit the headlines either in the Catholic or in the national newspapers.

It was precisely for this lack of publicity that Newman was blamed. What was the former Vicar of St Mary's doing, the man on whose lips the whole country had once hung? Why wasn't he receiving Lords and Duchesses into the Church as had been expected from him? Newman replied to these reproaches in a letter to his Community: 'If we are really doing a work, or rather many works, and all the complaint means is that we do not push and advertise it to the four corners of the earth, then I do but rejoice at it, as a mark, special and singular, of our being the children of St Philip. If there be one more than another, which is his gift and after his pattern, it is to live in the shade. . . . It is our great privilege, that we can work in many ways here and get no credit at all for it; and that first, because we are not seen, and next because those to whom we minister are persons of low estate, of whom the world thinks little. . . . I know well, that, as to myself, all through life, when I have been despised most, I have succeeded most: and I feel confident that to ask for scorn, contempt, slight, and the like treatment for my Congregation, is to ask for *great* success, *real* work, for fruits which are not unveiled here, in order that they may be reserved in all their freshness and bloom and perfection for manifestation at the marriage feast above.'

He told them, with the gentle sarcasm typical of him, that it was not necessary for members of the Oratory 'to talk fluently about its peculiar vocation', as the London House was constantly doing, but that it was 'of the utmost importance that every one of us should be formed upon it'. He knew that they were considered humdrum and unspiritual, and 'Mystical Theology . . . may be profitably pursued by those who are led to it; for virtue consists

. . . not in knowledge, but in practice', but if, as in the case of
the London Oratory, Mystical Theology was supposed to be the
only subject worthy of study and all else despised, this was a great
mistake. Finally he instructed his own priests how to behave in
this unfortunate controversy with the other community. 'Let me
caution you, my dear Fathers, most earnestly,' he urged them, 'to
be very much on your guard lest you show anything like warmth
or irritation of feeling towards the Fathers of the Oratory of
Brompton, or *concerning* them—in the presence of others. If I
wished to use a worldly argument to dissuade you from doing so,
I should simply tell you . . . that, if you did so, it would
at once be put down by the world to jealousy. But, to speak
in a better way, let me beg you to consider how few of the
Fathers there are really implicated in this act—so few that, it is
difficult not to go on exempting one after another till the whole
heap seems vanishing away. For myself, I have among them dear
private friends . . . who, I am confident, have never harboured
towards me any feeling which was not kind and respectful. I am
quite sure, that whatever has been done by the mass of them, has
been done inadvertently . . . as to the rest, I trust we shall have
grace given us to enable us ever to pray, that they may come
to a better mind, resolving ourselves to bear what they do against
us calmly, gravely, patiently, and, as far as is allowable, in silence.'
Surely this was the advice of a truly spiritual man.

Yet Newman was not 'spiritual' enough for Dalgairns, who did
not realize that humble work for Christ's poor is far more truly
'spiritual' than talks about mysticism in convent parlours accompanied by constant grumblings and intrigues against one's superior.
Dalgairns and the Fathers of the London Oratory were afraid of
intellectualism. Indeed, Dalgairns talked about Newman's respect
for an intellectual conviction as 'most amusing'—though in this
they were only in step with the majority of Catholics in their time
—while Newman, with his trust in the intellect if kept within its
proper limits, was more than a century in advance. In the end
Dalgairns went back to the London Oratory, which he had left
three years before to rejoin Newman, whom he venerated despite

all his intrigues against him. In the address Newman gave to the community after Dalgairns had left it he began, with characteristic humility, by blaming his own insufficiency: If Dalgairns had been under another superior, Newman thinks, he might have 'been a gain and an ornament to our Community, and nothing else. I know, my dear Fathers,' he continues, 'I am quite deficient in what the life of St Ignatius . . . ascribes to that great saint so justly, the art of government—one branch of which is, what I do not mean to speak invidiously about, when I call it, the art of management. I think another person *could* have managed Fr. Bernard. A person so amiable, so affectionate, so gentle, could have been led by the hand. . . .' Nevertheless, Newman realized only too well that this was not the whole story, and that for all the virtue there was in his former subject, he was not without grave faults, faults which were accentuated rather than diminished by the fact that he had made some progress in holiness. For, Newman told his community, 'No paradox is truer than this, that the higher we are in holiness, the more are we in danger of going wrong. I have been accustomed to compare the ascent to perfection to the mounting a high ladder. As the climber gets higher, the ladder dances under him—behold the state of a soul mounting towards heaven. I thus account for the wonderful falls of holy men—the utter shipwreck of ascetics—the heresies of grave and learned teachers—the delusions in which Satan enwraps souls which he cannot on the whole separate from God. This is why Saints are so few—they drop off as they get more likely to be Saints.'

This is the same teaching which the mystics, especially St John of the Cross, have expressed in slightly different forms. What Newman calls 'the ladder dances under him' the Carmelite saint called 'the dark night', both of the senses and, especially, of the spirit. For the greater the sanctity, the more insidious and subtle the temptations.

The temptation of Dalgairns was to prefer his own views to those of his superior, to think himself more spiritual than his community, and to despise any offices which were not directly 'spiritual', so that Newman had to continue: 'He was asking others to do what he had no wish at all to do himself. . . . He ever seemed to forget . . . that there were a variety of duties incumbent on the Fathers, quite as necessary as those of a lay brother who cooks the dinner or sweeps the corridor, and quite as unspiritual. He seemed to ignore the office of Father Minister and Father Treasurer,* and seemed to grudge their existence. The whole circle of duties connected with a mission, he ignored too. No one was to do a hundred things which were absolutely necessary, they were to be done, or the day could not be got through. But he was not to hear of them—he was to hear of nothing but of Confessions, and other directly religious occupations—and these he undertook himself. Fathers were idle, if they were not engaged in these.' Newman proposed an office to Dalgairns in which he could have done a great deal of good, but he refused it, because it was not sufficiently 'spiritual'. He complained of his duties as a guest master, of routine confessions, preferring more 'interesting' work in convents. In fact, he was ever restless, criticizing others and being excited because the community did not come up to his personal ideal. But, Newman says, 'One of the sure signs of the presence of the Spirit of God is peace. The Saints have gone through many fierce trials; I do not read that they were restless. . . . What men do calmly, has weight—but when they are restless, they seem to me to want the primary condition for inspiring confidence in others.'

Newman himself never lost his calm, even during the distressing months of the Achilli trial or in later years when one disappointment followed the other. For his spirituality penetrated his whole life; there was not one action more 'spiritual' than the other; whether he wrote a letter of spiritual direction, preached a university sermon or did accounts (he had always been remarkably good at figures), it was all done in the spirit of St Paul who wrote to the Corinthians: 'Whether you eat or drink, or whatever you do, do all to the glory of God.' This is spiritual maturity. It is, on the other hand, as the mystics tell us, a sign of spiritual im-

* Two offices concerned with the material needs of the community.

maturity to consider only 'devotional' practices to have religious value, a temptation to which the London house in the time of Faber and Dalgairns, who became superior after Faber's death, seems to have succumbed.

Newman's calm was put to severe tests, when all his efforts to do things for the Church were constantly rebuffed. First (in 1857) he was asked by Wiseman to undertake a new translation of the Bible, and he at once began to assemble staff, set a room apart in the house of the Birmingham Oratory and organize other pre-liminary measures. But when he tried to get definite answers on such essential questions as finance he received no reply, and finally he had to abandon the project. Next he undertook the editorship of the *Rambler*, a Catholic periodical which had got into hot water for expressing liberal views. Trying to save it, Newman did his best to change its tone, but a short sentence in his commentary on 'Contemporary Events' set in motion a sequence of events which led to the loss of his reputation in Rome and long years of isolation and frustration.

The paragraph in which the sentence occurred dealt with the problem of Catholic schools on which, Newman felt, the laity ought to be asked their opinion, for, he argued: 'If even in the preparation of a dogmatic definition the faithful are consulted, as lately in the instance of the Immaculate Conception, it is at least as natural to anticipate such an act of kind feeling and sym-pathy in great practical questions. . . .' The offensive word was 'consulted'. How could the laity, whose 'province' was, according to the outrageous remark of Mgr. Talbot, 'to hunt, to shoot, to entertain', how could the laity have any say in theological matters?

Instead of humbly apologizing for such a 'heretical' view New-man brought all his theological and historical guns into action and wrote an article in the July number of the *Rambler* with a title that was by itself to have the same effect on the English and Roman authorities as the proverbial red rag on the bull; for it was headed 'On Consulting the Faithful in Matters of Doctrine'. In it Newman first explained what he meant by 'consult', which he did not take in the Latin sense of seeking advice, but in the more ordinary English meaning of 'inquiring into a matter of *fact*', in the same way as one 'consults' a watch or a barometer. Then he analysed Church history and established with a wealth of quotations and erudition that during the Arian controversy in the fourth century it was not the bishops who preserved the true doctrine, because the large majority of them followed the Arian heresy which was supported by the Emperor, but the simple faithful who resisted the heresy and often even died for the true faith. The proofs he gave for this statement are overwhelming and are known to all students of the Patristic age, but, as has happened only too often in the history of the Church, facts that are distasteful to authority must be suppressed. It was somewhat naïve of Newman to have imagined that he could defend his views and convince his opponents by simply giving them the historical facts. On the contrary, he was delated to Rome and the Pope was said to be 'much hurt' (beaucoup peiné). In a letter to Wiseman Newman offered to explain his position, but Wiseman procrastinated as usual, and finally the matter blew over. Newman remained under a cloud and ceased to write for five years.

Strangely enough, it was the last paragraph of the article which had given particular offence, for there Newman had written: 'I think certainly that the *Ecclesia docens* [the teaching Church, i.e. Pope, Cardinals and Bishops] is more happy when she has such enthusiastic partisans about her as here represented [viz. in a description of the cheering crowds at Ephesus, after Mary had been proclaimed Theotokos—Mother of God—by the Council of 431] than when she cuts off the faithful from the study of her divine doctrines and the sympathy of her divine contemplations, and requires from them a *fides implicita* [implicit faith] in her word, which in the educated classes will terminate in indifference, and in the poorer in superstition.'

In view of the history of the Church in the later nineteenth and early twentieth centuries it is hardly necessary to emphasize how prophetic Newman's words were. How he would have rejoiced had he read in the Constitution on the Church of Vatican II that the laity, the 'People of God', 'are called upon, as living members, to expend all their energy for the growth of the Church and its continuous sanctification'. He himself wrote in a letter to Henry Wilberforce at the time of the *Rambler* controversy: 'I did all I could to ascertain God's Will, and, that being the case, I am sure good will come of my taking it. I am of opinion that the Bishops only see one side of things, and I have a mission, as far as my own internal feelings go, against evils which I *see*. On the other hand, I have always preached that things which are really useful, still are done, according to God's Will, at *one time, not at another*; and that, if you attempt at a *wrong* time, what in *itself* is *right*, you perhaps become a heretic or schismatic. What I may aim at may be real and good, but it may be God's Will it should be done a hundred years later.'

It certainly is being done now, more than a hundred years later, but whether it was actually God's will that Newman should not have been allowed to do it or whether it was only the stupidity and obstinacy of men who prevented its being done earlier is at least doubtful, seeing that the Church has lost so much ground through its refusal to liberalize itself and to educate its laity in Newman's spirit.

In the years which followed, Newman refrained from publishing anything, but contented himself with his everyday duties as superior of the Birmingham Oratory, to which a school had now been added. He took stock of his own spiritual development in some extremely revealing diary entries covering the years between the end of 1859 and the beginning of 1863, when his reputation as well as his mood were at their lowest. He begins by stating that he has 'less sensible devotion and inward life', and he traces this state to the fact that the fervour and energy of youth have gone; 'the same grace goes much further in youth, as encountering less opposition' he thinks. He had never made a deeper study of the great mystics, or he might have realized that the dryness by which he was affected, the discouragement and disgust are stages on the way towards closer union with God and in themselves greater graces than the emotional fervour of youth. But the very fact that he was prevented from realizing this was a further trial.

He then analyses his youthful spiritual aspirations which were discussed earlier in this book, when 'I prayed earnestly that I might not rise to any ecclesiastical dignity. . . . I knew what I was saying, and how it is Thy way to grant, to fulfil such petitions, and to take men at their word. . . . Yet I am not at all sure that grace had much to do with my wish . . . those prayers were immediately prompted, as I think, in great measure by natural rashness, generosity, cheerfulness, sanguine temperament, and unselfishness, though not, I trust, without Thy grace. I trust they were good and pleasing to Thee—but I much doubt, if I, my present self, just as I am, were set down in those past years, 1820, or 1822, or 1829, if they could be brought back, whether I now should make those good prayers and bold resolves, unless, that is, I had some vast and extraordinary grant of grace from Thy heavenly treasure-house.' Newman attributes his present unwillingness to make such generous prayers to old age, when the soul is 'half dead' and asks that God may rid him 'of this frightful *cowardice*. . . . When I was young, I was bold, because I was ignorant—now I have lost my boldness, because I have advanced in experience. I am able to count the cost, better than I did, of being brave for Thy sake, and therefore I shrink from sacrifices.'

But it was not only the experience of maturity that made him shrink from sacrifices which seemed easy to him in youth. After a lifetime of pondering on the dangers of the growing unbelief and having become fully aware of his own intellectual powers, Newman in his sixties knew what he could do for the Church, if he were but given a free hand. He knew that what was needed was his own unique combination of deep spirituality with clearsighted awareness of the trends of the times, a theology that was open to the world and a spirituality that rested on secure foundations. For, he writes in the same notes: 'To me conversions were not the first thing, but the edification [in the sense of 'building up'] of Catholics. So much have I fixed upon the latter as my object, that up to this time the world persists in saying that I recommend Protestants not to become Catholics. And, when I have given as my true opinion, that I am afraid to make hasty converts of educated men, lest they should not have counted the cost, and should have difficulties after they have entered the Church, I do but imply the same thing, that the Church must be prepared for converts, as well as converts prepared for the Church. . . . Catholics in England, from their very blindness, cannot see that they are blind. To aim then at improving the condition, the status, of the Catholic body, by a careful survey of their argumentative basis, of their position relative to the philosophy and the character of the day, by giving them juster views, by enlarging and refining their minds, in one word, by education, is (in their view) more than a superfluity or a hobby, it is an insult.'

The young tutor of Oriel and vicar of St Mary's had felt the need to insist to his sophisticated audiences on the dangers of 'accomplishments'; the Catholic priest, surrounded by prejudices, ignorance and superstition had to preach the opposite: the need of Catholics to be educated, so as to become a body that knew what it believed and why it believed and could defend the faith to the modern world, 'things', Newman writes, 'which I ought to have been specially suited to do, and have not done'—for his idea of the Irish University had ultimately come to nothing and his zeal for an educated laity was looked on as heretical.

The 'dark night of the soul', as St John of the Cross calls the trials by which God purifies a man for union with him, comes to different people in different ways; and usually in the ways that hurt this particular human being most. Newman had no need to be purified of attachment to material things or to such spiritual 'luxuries' as visions and sweet devotional feelings. But his great, his overwhelming desire was to be useful to the Church and do all he could to counteract the dangers of increasing unbelief and materialism which he saw so much more clearly than other English Catholics. And it was precisely in this most praiseworthy desire that he was continually mortified, and what hurt him most was that his opponents were not unbelievers or Protestants, but men of his own faith, particularly his superiors, of whom he wrote with deep disappointment: 'My Superiors, though they may claim

my obedience, have no claim on my admiration, and offer nothing
for my inward trust.' a mind of his own.

And as the 'dark night' is commonly accompanied by temptations so it was also in Newman's case; and his temptation was to
look back, back on the time when, as an Anglican, he was the
most influential preacher in Oxford, indeed in all England, when
young men were drawn to him and owed him their religious
beliefs. And just then this influence, which he had lost immediately after his conversion, was making itself felt again, and 'Those
very books and labours of mine, which Catholics did not understand, Protestants did. . . . Hence some sympathy is showing
itself towards me on the part of certain persons, who have deliberately beat me down and buried me for the last ten years. And
accordingly I have been attracted by that sympathy to desire more
of that sympathy, feeling lonely, and fretting under, not so much
the coldness towards me (though that in part) as the ignorance,
narrowness of mind, and self conceit of those, whose faith and
virtue and goodness, nevertheless, I at the same time recognized.
And thus I certainly am under the temptation of looking out for,
if not courting, Protestant praise.' A few years before, during a
stormy passage from England to Ireland, Newman had recorded
a strange dream to Ambrose St John: 'Think of a Parson getting
into my birth (*sic*), and threatening my face with his feet; and
my resolving to convert him; and choosing as my instrument a
glass jar of large preserved gooseberries; and failing, because he
found them undeniably full of large maggots!' Newman evidently
only found it funny, for Freud was still more than half a century
in the future—but might it not well be interpreted as springing
from an awareness that there were many unpleasant features in
the Church—maggots—that prevented conversions? And might
it not also be an expression of Newman's own constant frustration
in all he undertook?

It was a very painful test for Newman, to find understanding
outside his own Church which he did not find within it, and he
can hardly be blamed for having felt some pleasure in it. He put
the matter in a nutshell: 'As a Protestant, I felt my religion

dreary, but not my life—but, as a Catholic, my life dreary, not my religion.' 'The Blessed Sacrament is my great consolation,' he wrote, and he realized that, after all, the trials that had come upon him were themselves but the answer to this lifelong prayer that he 'should be set aside in this world.' Now he had fully experienced what this meant to him and what sufferings it entailed, and with this knowledge he reiterated it, but in a somewhat different form: 'O Lord, bless what I write and prosper it—let it do much good, let it have much success; but let no praise come to me on that account in my lifetime.' If ever prayer was prophetic this was. It was written in 1860. Almost exactly a century later John XXIII announced the Second Vatican Council of which it is hardly too much to say that the spirit of Newman is evident in many of its most important documents.

7 THE DARKEST YEARS

BETWEEN 1859, when the article on 'Consulting the Laity' appeared and the *Apologia* in 1864, Newman did not write any books, but lived very quietly in Birmingham, occupied with his ordinary duties as an Oratorian and the school of the Oratory, which he had founded. He felt himself very much 'under a cloud', and as all his undertakings so far had come to nothing and, worse, he was even suspected of something like heresy, he kept silence. But this in itself was a severe trial; for he saw ever more clearly how much educational work was needed if the Church was to hold its own in the modern world, and how much the Catholic religion suffered from the lack of understanding on the part of its leaders. This urgent concern for the Church was behind so many of his utterances which sounded sometimes merely like personal grouses and were so interpreted. His state of mind in these dark years is most clearly expressed in two letters to an old friend of his, Emily Bowles, for a number of years a nun of Cornelia Connelly's Congregation of the Holy Child, which she later left after a quarrel with the foundress. To her Newman wrote in May 1863:

'To myself I feel as full of thought and life as ever I was—but a certain invisible chain impedes me, or bar stops me, when I attempt to do anything—and the only reason why I do not *enjoy* the happiness of being out of conflict is because I feel to myself I could do much in it.' This is the crux of the matter. 'All those questions of the day,' he continues, 'which make so much noise now—Faith and Reason, Inspiration, etc., etc.—would have been, according to my ability, worked out or fairly opened. Of course, I required elbow-room—but this was impossible.' And he goes on to say that in former times burning questions were freely discussed by theologians in the Universities, and Rome was only the ultimate court of appeal, after a subject had been thoroughly aired in free controversy. But '*now*, if I, as a private priest, put anything into print, Propaganda answers me at once. How can I fight with such a chain on my arm?' Not that he was particularly keen on fighting; on the contrary, when he came to Birmingham, 'I deliberately gave myself to a life of obscurity, which in my heart I love best. . . . And I am not only content, but really pleased that so things are. Yet there are those considerations which from time to time trouble me. First, lest my being where I am is my own doing in any measure, for then I say: "Perhaps I am hiding my talent in a napkin." Next, people say to me: "Why are you not doing more? How much you could do"; and then, since I think I could do a great deal if I were let to it, I become uneasy. And lastly, willing as I am to observe St Philip's dear rule that we "should despise being despised"; yet when I find that scorn and contempt become the means of my Oratory being injured, as they have before now, then I get impatient.'

During that decisive illness in Sicily more than thirty years before Newman had felt that he had a work to do in the Church of England, and that God was preserving him for that. Now, again, he felt 'that I have not yet fulfilled my mission and have work to do'. But this work was constantly hindered by those who ought to have encouraged it, and this produced in Newman those feelings of frustration that were also his own personal purification. That he realized this himself is evident from a poem, 'The Two Worlds', written in 1862:

> Unveil, O Lord, and on us shine
> In glory and in grace,
> This gaudy world grows pale before
> The beauty of Thy face.
>
> Till Thou art seen, it seems to be
> A sort of fairy ground,
> Where suns unsetting light the sky,
> And flowers and fruits abound.

But when Thy keener, purer beam
Is pour'd upon our sight,
It loses all its power to charm,
And what was day is night.

Its noblest toils are then the scourge
Which made Thy blood to flow;
Its joys are but the treacherous thorns
Which circled round Thy brow.

And thus, when we renounce for Thee
Its restless aims and fears,
The tender memories of the past,
The hopes of coming years,

Poor is our sacrifice, whose eyes
Are lighted from above;
We offer what we cannot keep,
What we have ceased to love.

A contemplative makes this renunciation of the world outwardly once and for all, and his temptations and sufferings come, first, from inward desires to go back on it in some way or other, and later from trials in the life of prayer, interior desolation, feelings of being forsaken by God as well as by external sufferings from misunderstandings, loss of friends, defamation and so forth. But an educator like Newman could not give up the world once and for all; he had by his very vocation to take part in it, to study it, to make use of all the possibilities of influencing it. This produced an inevitable tension between his quite genuine desire to 'live in obscurity, out of the world and the world's thoughts' in the presence of Jesus, Mary and Joseph, as he expresses it in one of his Meditations, and his equally genuine conviction that he had a special vocation to be active in solving the problems the Church had to face in the modern world. In the light of divine contemplation all this appeared to be futile, 'restless aims and fears' that were but a poor sacrifice compared with the glory of the Lord— and yet, if seen from the point of view of the Church as it is here and now it was of the greatest importance. This is why he could write in a moment of profound dejection: 'What am I living for? what am I doing for any religious end?'

His spiritual life at this time, too, seems mostly to have been lived in the state of the 'dark night'. In his 'Meditations on Christian Doctrine', some of which were probably written during these years, he prays: 'My God and Saviour . . . take not from *me* the light of Thy Countenance, lest I shrivel from the loss of it and perish in my infirmity. . . . Who can walk without light, or labour without the pure air, but Thy great Saints? As for me, alas, I shall turn to the creature for my comfort, if Thou wilt not give me Thyself. I shall not mourn, I shall not hunger or thirst after justice, but I shall look about for whatever is at hand, and feed on offal. . . . O my God, leave me not in that dry state in which I am; give me the comfort of Thy grace. How can I have any tenderness or sweetness, unless I have Thee to look upon? how can I continue in prayer . . . unless Thou encourage me and make it pleasant to me? It is hardly that an old man keeps any warmth in him. . . .'

As we saw earlier on, with increasing age Newman found it more difficult to pray, because he had no longer the fervour of youth. In these years when he felt abandoned and useless, the seeming absence of God weighed heavily on him. He confessed that he often found it difficult 'even to say my prayers. . . . Give me grace, O my Father, to be utterly ashamed of my own reluctance. . . . Teach me to love meditation, sacred reading, and prayer.' The very fact that he suffered from this apparent inability to pray shows that this was a spiritual trial through which he had to pass, not a defect of his own personal life. But such outcries, as well as his complaints about the authorities that fettered him, have led to the wide-spread opinion that Newman did not have the makings of a saint. St Teresa of Avila had said: 'To suffer or to die', and in the traditional lives of the saints one reads that they bore the most atrocious sufferings without a murmur, indeed welcomed humiliations and opposition of all kinds. But did they? And would they have been human if they did? Even Christ himself agonized in the garden of Gethesemane, St Paul had hard words for the 'pseudo-apostles' who hindered his work, and for all her love of suffering St Teresa complained a good deal when she had to leave her beloved Castile and go to Andalusia, where she did not like the people. Hardly any saints have left such an enormous volume of correspondence as Newman, and most of their letters which have survived are of spiritual direction, not quite personal outpourings. On the other hand, the great Doctors of the early Church—St Jerome, St John Chrysostom, St Cyril of Alexandria, St Augustine—to whom Newman may well be compared, have never been forced into the straitjacket of a modern canonization process, through which they would hardly have come successfully. These theological giants complained, intrigued, attacked, and they were proclaimed saints because of their great services to the Church. But today it is very much easier for a foundress of one of the innumerable women's congregations to be canonized, whose life was strictly circumscribed and whose correspondence is of no interest, than for an original and far-seeing thinker whose writings are of the greatest value to the Church and whose life was completely given to the service of God and his neighbour, but who, being a man, sometimes gave way to despondency and complaints.

Newman was anxious that the Church should present an image attractive, not repellent to modern men. Now the saints are, as it were, the 'advertisement' of the Church's holiness. Why then are there so few modern saints that appeal to men and women of our time? It is not that holiness itself is repellent to our contemporaries, but only a certain type of it. Saints like Thomas More, a man like Pope John are very popular; why cannot the Church canonize more men (and women) like these, full-blooded human beings who are aware of the needs of their time, of the problems of their contemporaries? Humility and obedience—which Newman, for one, certainly possessed—are, indeed, great Christian virtues, but they are not the only ones. The apostles had initiative, the great doctors an intellect geared to the defence and elaboration of the faith, men like St Thomas Aquinas (who, incidentally, was

accused of heresy in his lifetime) the gift to combine the new
philosophy of his age with the traditions of the Church—but they
were not constantly harassed by suspicion as Newman was, they
had the 'elbow room' which he so sorely missed. And because he
complained of the lack of this essential element for the development of the human, including the Christian, intellect, he was
considered a grumbler whose virtue and theology were equally
suspect. His theology has been justified by now, but a cloud still
seems to hang over his character, simply because it does not agree
with the stereotyped image of sanctity still prevalent in the post-
Tridentine Catholic Church. Certainly Newman himself thought
that he was very far from being a saint—but which saint (apart
from a few exceptions like St Teresa of Lisieux who foresaw her
own canonization) has ever considered himself one? Which saint
has not accused himself of his sins and failings, often in very
exaggerated terms? Why should Newman's self-accusations be
taken more seriously than those of other holy men and women?
And that he found prayer difficult in his then state of constant
anxiety is not surprising. Combined with his enforced intellectual
inactivity the felt 'absence' of God was, indeed, hard to bear, but
as if this were not enough, Newman had now trouble also with
his own beloved Oratory at Birmingham. This arose over a quarrel
between Nicholas Darnell, headmaster of the Oratory School, and
Mrs Wootten, its matron, with whose work Darnell interfered.
Darnell behaved in a very high-handed manner without any
regard to the fact that Newman was his superior and the school
belonged to him. He resigned almost immediately, taking the
secular masters with him, and Newman had to spend considerable time trying to find replacements. Moreover, another member
of the community, Stanislas Flanagan, also became unsettled and
left not long afterwards, so that the already small Birmingham
community was sadly depleted.

Newman's sufferings under this string of disappointments
showed even in his face: 'How am I changed even in look!' he
wrote in his diary. 'Till the affair of No. 90 and my going to
Littlemore, I had my mouth half open, and commonly a smile

on my face—and from that time onwards my mouth has been closed and contracted, and the muscles are so set now, that I cannot but look grave and forbidding. . . . *Now*, I am so conscious of my own stern look, that I hardly like to see people. It began when I set my face towards Rome; and since I made the great sacrifice, to which God called me, He has rewarded me in ten thousand ways, O how many! but he has marked my course with almost unintermittent mortification.' The worst of it was that, in the nature of the case, Newman could not fight back. He could not attack the Roman authorities, he could not lay before the world the troubles in his own community, though his opponents had no such qualms and were spreading all kinds of rumours.

In a letter written about this time he poured out his heart: 'It is so bad to be simply passive in suffering. When we act as well as suffer, the effort alleviates the pain; in that case men are wounded without knowing it, but it is otherwise when you are hit, without hitting. It would have been better with me, humanly and naturally, had I given as good as I took.' He then records his many disappointments and the frequent attacks on him: 'These are little and ridiculous things taken separately, but they form a sort of atmosphere of *flies*—one can't enjoy a walk without this fidget on the nerves of the mind. They are nothing in the eye of reason, but they weary.' Then he outlines the struggle between the supernatural aspect of his sufferings and his natural reactions: 'I think of Keble's lines "In disappointment Thou canst bless" and I know that it is better far for me to seem to have done nothing—but still it is most difficult to go on working in the face of thirty years disappointment. And so it is—everything seems to crumble under my hands, as if one were making ropes of sand. I am speaking of the *physical* effects of such a trial. I suppose supernatural acts of whatever kind, are the destruction of flesh and blood. Do you think the *sollicitudo omnium Ecclesiarum* [the care of all the Churches] did not waste St Paul.' By 'care' is meant that mental burden which consists in the perception of evil with the consciousness one cannot avert it. The wounds which one bears speechlessly, the dreadful secrets which are severed from the sym-

pathy of others, the destruction of confidences, the sense of hollowness all around one, the expectation of calamity or scandal, this
was a portion of St Paul's trial, and of all Bishops, as it is of all, in
their degree, who have to work for God in this world. It is as real
a penance as a hair shirt.

'And as one man's skin endures a hair shirt better than another's
so it is with the effect of these trials on different minds respec-
tively. For myself, I know I am deeply deficient in that higher
life which lasts and grows in spite of the ills of mortality—but had
I ever so much of supernatural love and devotion, I could not be
in any different state from the Apostle, who in the most beautiful
of his inspired epistles speaks with such touching and consoling
vividness of those troubles, in the midst of which these earthen
vessels of ours hold the treasures of grace and truth.'

Newman has from time to time been accused of over-sensitive-
ness, of grumbling too much, of not exhibiting that joy which is
the hallmark of sanctity. But these criticisms show both a defec-
tive view of Newman's character and a far too narrow concept of
sanctity. It is quite true that Newman was not 'tough' but had
the sensitivity almost indispensable in a scholar. But surely
this is not a fault? On the contrary, Stoicism is not a Christian virtue. It is only natural that a person should feel frustrated
if he is prevented from doing the work for Christ which he feels
called to do. That Newman complained fairly often of being so
constantly thwarted is no sign of deficient spirituality either. For
just these descriptions in his notes and letters show the intense
inner struggle between supernatural acceptance of pain and natural
psychological reactions to it, which has been the lot of all great
Christians. The 'destruction of flesh and blood', as Newman calls
it, causes intense suffering; Newman describes it in terms that fit
every saint, but have a special reference to himself: the secrets
'which are severed from the sympathy of others' refer no doubt to
the Oratorian difficulties which he could not make known to
friends outside his community; the 'destruction of confidence, the
sense of hollowness all around one, the expectation of calamity
or scandal' is a description of his position in the Church, suspected

by Rome and slandered by so many English Catholics as he then was. But then, after accusing himself of deficiency in that 'higher life' that upheld the saints in all their troubles, he gives voice to his innermost conviction that, despite everything, he is yet in the same situation as St Paul, holding 'the treasures of grace and truth' even though in 'earthen vessels'.

It is significant that Newman should call 2 Corinthians, from which these words are taken, the most beautiful of St Paul's epistles. For it is the letter in which the apostle speaks most freely of himself, in which he details his sufferings in the service of Christ, in which he even mentions his own mystical experiences and 'boasts' of his own apostolic qualifications as opposed to those of the false teachers who had made such an impression on the Corinthians.

Newman certainly does not wish to compare his sufferings and his work for Christ with those of the apostle. What he does mean is that even St Paul bore his apostolic grace in an 'earthen vessel', that he, too, yearned for understanding and sympathy with his troubles, that he suffered when he was misrepresented and said so. And if Newman's 'pain threshold' lay low, if he was perhaps more sensitive to slights and failures than more robust natures, surely this does not detract from his holiness. For the other side of this 'sensitivity' was his understanding of others, his sympathy and his extraordinary gift for friendship, which made even those who had opposed and injured him in the end accuse themselves rather than him. This had been evident at the Achilli trial, when the Judge himself had misgivings about his 'lecturing' Newman, this was the case with Darnell, who wrote a few years later that his conduct to Newman had been 'ungrateful and ungracious'. And when in 1863 Faber, who had been so great a trial to Newman, was on his death bed, Newman described their last meeting thus: 'He said he had loved me the best of any one in the world, next to the late Duke of Norfolk. He said a sermon of mine at St Mary's had been the turning point of his life. . . . He said that it had pained him much to think that he and his were adding to my many trials.' But Faber described Newman's own manner:

'No woman could be tenderer than he was—the whole interview was effusive of more than kindness, of downright love—all is right and righter than right. We held each other's hand the whole while, and talked about our old friendship . . . you would have been strangely moved had you seen his face when he came to leave and looked down upon me and said in a voice of the most consummate sweetness "St Philip be with you, Father".'

Yet, despite this tenderness Newman himself continued his notes on this last interview: 'My own view about Faber, poor fellow, is not much changed by the above. It is quite certain that he has from time to time spoken against me. . . . But all through . . . he was, as it were, arguing with himself that he had not been unkind to me; rather than boldly saying he had ever been a hearty friend. . . .'

At first sight it may seem incongruous that Newman should have been so tender at their meeting, yet so stern and at the same time somewhat patronizing, 'Faber, poor fellow' when he wrote the account of it afterwards. And in view of such a complicated attitude it is, perhaps, not surprising that despite his utter sincerity Newman should sometimes have been accused of duplicity and even been nicknamed 'the serpent'. But the fact of the matter seems to have been that Newman and his friends and Faber and his circle were two quite different types of character that found it very difficult to understand each other. Newman always separated objective truth from personal feelings. He could have feelings of affection for a person, yet not trust him, because this person had disappointed him too often. Newman certainly pitied Faber, and for the sake of past friendship as well as Christian charity he did all he could to make the dying man happy. But this did not blind him to his faults and to the estrangement that had been between them. Faber, on the other hand, lived by his emotions, and he could not understand why Newman should not accept his protestations of love at their face value, even if Faber's actions contradicted them. For to Faber emotions were at least as real as actions, if not perhaps more so, and so he was hurt when Newman rejected them. It was one of the tragic features of Newman's life that he should attract these emotional converts irresistibly, yet repel them by his enormous intellectual superiority. For their letters make their admiration for him quite plain; Dalgairns himself wrote 'How very small I feel beside him'—and it was probably just this feeling of smallness he gave them quite unconsciously that impelled them to hurt him even against their better judgement.

Newman had once written: 'Faith ought to be tried and tested, if it *be* faith. I don't like that faith, which (as I have seen written to a new convert), is a "precious tender plant", to be sedulously guarded under a glass cover, or in a hothouse—and exotic—if so our religion is a mere "alien religion", an "Oriental faith and worship"—but it is a tough principle within us, bearing heavy weights and hard work, or it is worth very little.' His own faith certainly was this, and during these years of silence and misunderstanding, during which he was even believed by some to be on his way back to the Church of England, it was being tested and tried, but never found wanting. In 1862 he had to contradict the story published in the *Lincolnshire Express* and reproduced in the *Globe* newspaper according to which he had 'become utterly sceptical' and was in the habit of ridiculing 'the Romish persuasion altogether'. Feeling that only the very strongest denial would quash these rumours he wrote to the *Globe*: 'I have not had one moment's wavering of trust in the Catholic Church ever since I was received into her fold. I hold, and ever have held, that her Sovereign Pontiff is the centre of unity and the Vicar of Christ; and I have ever had, and have still, an unclouded faith in her creed in all its articles; a supreme satisfaction in her worship, discipline and teaching; and an eager longing, and a hope against hope, that the many dear friends whom I have left in Protestantism may be partakers of my happiness. This being my state of mind, to add, as I hereby go on to do, that I have no intention, and never had any intention, of leaving the Catholic Church . . . would be superfluous, except that Protestants are always on the look-out for some loophole in a Catholic's statement of fact. Therefore . . . I do hereby profess *ex animo* . . . that Protestantism is the dreariest of possible religions; that the thought of the Anglican service makes me shiver, and the thought of the Thirty-nine Articles makes me shudder.' He expressed himself so strongly because he realized that otherwise the rumours would continue, and he assured his old friends in the Church of England that he would not have hurt them if it had not been absolutely necessary to make his position clear. Eighteen months later he wrote the book that was not only to break his long silence but also to restore his reputation.

8 *THE APOLOGIA* AND *THE DREAM OF GERONTIUS*

THE story of the *Apologia pro Vita Sua* is well known. Charles Kingsley, a clergyman of the Church of England and author of the popular children's book *The Water Babies,* had written in a review published in *Macmillan's Magazine* in January 1864: 'Truth for its own sake had never been a virtue with the Roman clergy. Father Newman informs us that it need not be, and on the whole ought not to be', an assertion Kingsley pretended to find in Newman's sermon on 'Wisdom and Innocence' (incidentally one of his Anglican *Sermons on Subjects of the Day*). A lively controversy ensued, and at last, in order once and for all to prove that he had always acted truthfully and in accordance with the demands of his conscience Newman decided to write the 'History of his Religious Opinions' which led to his becoming a Catholic. The book was written at a terrific speed in weekly instalments, beginning on April 21 and ending on June 12. The strain was tremendous: 'I have been constantly in tears, and constantly crying out in distress', as he wrote to a friend in May. For as he wrote he lived once more through his own youth, his friendships, all his joys and all his disappointments, his whole intellectual and religious development; it was like the katharsis in a Greek drama, a crisis that operated a final purification, both in the chief actor and in his audience. Newman took stock of his own life, and those who read his book could see him as he really was. In chapter V, which he called 'Position of my Mind since 1845' he made his confession of Faith which is very important to the subject of this book. In it he says that since his conversion to Catholicism he has 'had no anxiety of heart whatever. I have been in perfect peace and contentment; I never have had one doubt . . . it was like coming into port after a rough sea; and my happiness on that score remains to this day without interruption.' Throughout all these troubled years he had been at peace with himself; he had never doubted that the Catholic Church was the true Church; he was supremely happy in his religion.

But Newman was a modern, not a medieval Christian; for him as for us faith is beset with difficulties. Yet 'Ten thousand difficulties do not make one doubt, as I understand the subject; difficulty and doubt are incommensurate.' And the greatest difficulty of all is the being of God, 'and yet borne in upon our minds with most power'. 'If I looked into a mirror, and did not see my face,' Newman continues, 'I should have the sort of feeling which actually comes upon me, when I look into this living busy world, and see no reflexion of its Creator. This is to me, one of those great difficulties of this absolute primary truth. . . . Were it not for this voice, speaking so clearly in my conscience and my heart, I should be an atheist, or a pantheist, or a polytheist when I looked into the world.' The traditional proofs of the existence of God had little relevance for Newman, as little as they have for the majority of our contemporaries. But he had, what so many of us have not, a keen sense of the invisible world and of 'a profound mystery, which is absolutely beyond human solution'. And thus he did find a solution to the 'heart-piercing, reason-bewildering fact' of being unable to find God in the world, 'Either,' he says, 'there is no Creator, or this living society of men is in a true sense discarded from His presence. . . . And so I argue about the world—*if* there be a God, *since* there is a God, the human race is implicated in some terrible aboriginal calamity'. This calamity is what theologians call 'original sin'; it has affected the whole human being, including the intellect, and hence the Church tells us: 'your whole nature must be reborn . . . and, the last not the least, your intellect'.

But the intellect must be 're-born', it must not be killed. 'The energy of the human intellect' writes Newman, 'does from opposition grow'; it thrives and is joyous, with a tough elastic strength, under the terrible blows of the divinely-fashioned weapon [i.e. of infallibility], and is never so much itself as when it has lately been overthrown.' For infallibility itself is rigidly circumscribed, 'It is a supply for a need, and it does not go beyond that need. Its object is, and its effect also, not to enfeeble the freedom or vigour of human thought in religious speculation, but to resist and control its extravagance.' It is this extravagance that leads men to infidelity if it be not checked, and this is why the Church has to interfere from time to time to prevent the excesses of unaided reason. This, of course, applies only to the sphere of religion, not to that of secular science, over which the Church has no authority.

Thus Newman is led from the voice of conscience that proclaims his Creator to the acceptance of the infallible Church in which he found peace—not the peace of an intellectual graveyard, but the harmony that is found in the balancing of tensions. The book itself helped to ease the psychological tensions that had been set up by the failure to understand Newman on the part of both Catholics and Protestants, and especially of his ecclesiastical superiors. In February 1865 he wrote in his diary that the position of his mind now was so different from that which he had described two years before 'that it would require many words to bring it out'. He had got 'hardened against the opposition . . . from the natural effect of time', Cardinal Wiseman and Faber had been removed, though their place was now taken by Manning and Ward, author of *The Ideal of the Christian Church* and an extreme Ultramontane, and lastly there was the success of the *Apologia*, which he called 'a most wonderful deliverance . . . in my favour'. For through the *Apologia*, 'while I have regained, or rather gained, the favour of Protestants, I have received the approbation, in formal addresses of good part of the English clerical body'. These three factors, and most of all perhaps the success of the *Apologia*, brought about a new serenity, what spiritual writers call a 'holy indifference' that could view with equanimity not only future storms and stresses but death itself. It produced what is, at least in the view of the present writer, Newman's most beautiful and profound poem, *The Dream of Gerontius*.

It was written in January 1865, in the course of a few days, as the result of a sudden inspiration. Many Catholic mystics and spiritual writers have written about purgatory, frequently in very imaginative and frightening terms. Characteristically, *The Dream of Gerontius* is not about purgatory, but describes in dramatic form the moment between dying and appearing before the judgement seat of God. It expresses all Newman's awareness of the unseen world, and in its blending of philosophy, theology and poetry may well be compared to the hymns of St Thomas Aquinas. Newman himself had been pronounced to be near to death only a few months before, he had undergone the purification of great suffering, and thus it is perhaps not surprising that in this poem he often uses instinctively the terminology of later mystics whom he seems never to have read.

The moment of dying is described as a 'strange innermost abandonment', an 'emptying out of each constituent and natural force',

> As though my very being had given way,
> As though I was no more a substance now,
> And could fall back on nought to be my stay . . .
> And drop from out the universal frame
> Into that shapeless, scopeless, blank abyss,
> That utter nothingness, of which I came.

This is the mystics' language of the dark night—nought, shapeless, abyss, nothingness are all expressions used by them for their experience of the intense sufferings that precede the mystical union. It would be more than surprising, almost unbelievable, that Newman should have used this language which was unfamiliar to him to describe an experience of which he knew nothing. Moreover, his description is so vivid, so intense, that it must reflect a spiritual experience that had come to him, too, and which he objectified in this poem—for he seems no longer to have kept spiritual diaries as he had done in his younger days—and which may, perhaps, have also been too intimate to be expressed in other than objective terms. This experience of the void is horrifying, it weakens a man so that he has no longer even the 'strength to pray' but has to rely on the intercession of others.

The description of emptiness is followed by the prayers of the assistants and by Gerontius' own confession of faith:

> And I hold in veneration
> For the love of Him alone,
> Holy Church, as His creation,
> And her teachings, as His own.
> And I take with joy whatever
> Now besets me, pain or fear,
> And with a strong will I sever
> All the ties which bind me here.

The Catholic mystics have always built their spiritual life on the doctrines of the Church, even though they were, like Newman, from time to time in opposition to some of the Church's official representatives. For they, like Newman, did not see in the Church primarily a human institution, though it is also that, but the creation of Christ, who taught and still teaches through it.

But after this firm confession of faith Gerontius is once more given over to the terrors of death,

> That sense of ruin, which is worse than pain,
> That masterful negation and collapse
> Of all that makes me man; as though I bent
> Over the dizzy brink
> Of some sheer infinite descent;
> Or worse, as though
> Down, down for ever I was falling through
> The solid framework of created things,
> And needs must sink and sink
> Into the vast abyss. . . .

Now the language of the mystics mingles with another: the sense of ruin, collapse, the dizzy brink—this is the language of existential *angst*, the modern man's horror of the nothingness that seems to await him after death which is so characteristic of

L

Kierkegaard, who had to take the 'leap' into faith to save him from despair. Newman, who had known this feeling when he looked into a world that did not reflect its Creator, knew well the horror that must come to man when even this world melts away and he is left face to face with the vast abyss of nothingness. But for him, the Christian, there is even worse than that:

> Some bodily form of ill
> Floats on the wind, with many a loathsome curse
> Tainting the hallow'd air, and laughs, and flaps
> Its hideous wings,
> And makes me wild with horror and dismay.

The forces of evil, so little acknowledged in ordinary life, become very real both to the mystic in his hours of temptation and to the every-day Christian in the hour of death, when they show themselves in all their hideousness. In the dark years that preceded the *Apologia* Newman must sometimes have felt them, when he asked himself in near-despair, 'What am I living for', and looked back nostalgically on his Anglican days so full of vigour and optimism.

But then, suddenly, the dark night is over. Death has come; to Gerontius natural death, to Newman that spiritual death to all worldly ambition, even the ambition to work for the Church, which leaves man in profound peace, the state of spiritual fulfilment that the 'soul of Gerontius' expresses in beautiful language which again seems to echo a deep inner experience:

> . . . I feel in me
> An inexpressive lightness, and a sense
> Of freedom, as I were at length myself,
> And ne'er had been before.

The freedom the soul feels after death is similar to that of the mystic once the dark night is over, when the troubles of this world matter so much less than before, because he has gained his liberty and is now the true self God meant him to be.

Newman then meditates on the way in which the soul leaves this world:

> So much I know, not knowing how I know,
> That the vast universe, where I have dwelt,
> Is quitting me, or I am quitting it.
> Or I or it is rushing on the wings
> Of light or lightning on an onward course,
> And we e'en now are million miles part.
> Yet . . . is this peremptory severance
> Wrought out in lengthening measurements of space
> Which grow and multiply by speed and time?
> Or am I traversing infinity
> By endless subdivision, hurrying back
> From finite towards infinitesimal,
> Thus dying out of the expansive world?

Here speaks the modern thinker, philosophizing about the relations between speed, time and space. Where earlier Christians found no difficulty in letting the soul simply jump, as it were, from this world into the next, Newman was aware of the problems of linking time to eternity, the man who had lived in the universe to the soul existing outside time and space. He just asks the question in what way this may come about and offers some theories, he does not pretend to solve the problem.

Then the soul becomes aware of its guardian angel—'Someone has me fast within his ample palm'—whose task is now over and who has come to take the soul home. Some of the songs of the angels are among the most beautiful parts of the poem, and here the patristic inspiration is very clear, when the guardian angel, praising God in his wonderful creature, Man, 'strange composite of heaven and earth', says that he is 'to fill the thrones which angels lost through pride'; for as early as the second-century Justin the Martyr, the Greek Fathers held that man was created to occupy the places which the fallen angels had vacated in heaven. In Newman's poem the angels themselves are hierarchic intellectual beings, resembling those awe-inspiring figrures of the early mosaics rather than the charming creatures of the late medieval painters like Fra Angelico. When the soul asks its guardian angel why it is not yet at the throne of God, the angel instructs it on the absence of time; what seems a long time to it since it left the body is in reality less than a 'million-million-millionth part' of 'a moment, as men measure time'; for 'in the immaterial world . . . intervals in their succession are measured by the living thought alone'; thus it is no external hindrance, but

> It is thy very energy of thought
> Which keeps thee from thy God.

This explanation that eternity is measured by the 'energy of thought' removes the danger of conceiving it as an endless succession of time, a very anthropomorphic idea which has led many modern critics of Christianity to reject the very concept of eternity. The disembodied soul is prevented from encountering God immediately neither by space nor by time, but by the energy of its thought which has not yet left the earthly life completely behind. The instructions of the guardian angel prepare it for the divine presence, but the soul is not ready for it yet. It has still to pass through the 'middle region', the sphere of the demonic powers, which Newman endows with 'the high thought, and the glance of fire, of the great spirits . . . the mind bold and independent, the purpose free', surely a reflexion of that unbridled freedom of thought that was the 'liberalism' of his time, with its power of seducing the minds of men away from the faith.

The soul is surprised that it is no longer afraid of these powers of evil, but rather despises them, and the angel explains that in its 'trial-state' it had 'a traitor nestling close at home', the sinful inclinations 'connatural' to it, which were in league with the powers of hell and hence appeared so terrifying. But they were powerless when faced with sanctity, as in the case of the 'holy hermit in his cell', whose prowess in the face of Satan was described in the lives of St Antony and other Desert Fathers which Newman knew so well.

The soul hears the demons as it hears its angel, but is puzzled
that it does not see them; it is a question that bears also on the
problem of the knowledge of the disembodied souls in heaven.
It is strange that Newman did not solve it by means of the 'spiritual senses' which, according to Origen and other Fathers, were
developed by 'spiritual men' as they approached perfection and
enabled them to understand and converse with the spiritual world.
Newman probably felt that they were so strongly attached to the
living person as a counterpart of the physical senses that they, too,
had no place in the disembodied soul. Instead, the angel explains
that though the soul imagines itself still to have touch, taste or
hearing, it does not actually have these but merely remains aware
of them as a man whose hand or foot has been severed still
imagines to have feeling in them. For now, in this moment between death and eternal life, the soul lives 'in a world of signs and
types' and being weaned from the material world, is 'swathed
around in dreams, dreams that are true, yet enigmatical', for it
can grasp the truths of the immaterial world as yet only through
symbols. It is blind until it is given the Beatific Vision, and 'even
thy purgatory, which comes like fire, is fire without its light.'
   The soul accepts this, but says it has always believed

> That, ere I plunged amid the avenging flame,
> I had one sight of Him to strengthen me.

The angel confirms this belief, but he warns the soul that it
does not know what it asks:

> . . . that sight of the Most Fair
> Will gladden thee, but it will pierce thee too . . .
> Learn that the flame of the Everlasting Love
> Doth burn ere it transform. . . .

From his earliest days Newman had opposed the easy-going
religion of his time which pictured God as a kind grandfather.
As we have seen, as a Catholic he began to stress the love of God
more than he had done as an Anglican. But the more his own

spiritual life developed, the more he became aware of the infinite
holiness of God in relation to sinful man, a holiness that was both
the ineffable joy and the intense pain of man. Before this divine
love can transform it must burn—this is the teaching of all the
mystics, who place the intense sufferings of mystical love before
what they call the 'transforming union'.

Then the angel instructs Gerontius still further, and these verses
must be quoted at length, because they show so clearly that Newman can have been no stranger to mystical experience.

> It is the face of the Incarnate God
> Shall smite thee with that keen and subtle pain;
> And yet the memory which it leaves will be
> A sovereign febrifuge to heal the wound;
> And yet withal it will the wound provoke,
> And aggravate and widen it the more.

And he continues a few lines further on:

> When then—if such thy lot—thou seest thy Judge . . .
> Thou wilt be sick with love, and yearn for Him . . .
> There is a pleading in His pensive eyes
> Will pierce thee to the quick, and trouble thee.
> And thou wilt hate and loathe thyself; for though
> Now sinless, thou wilt feel that thou hast sinn'd
> As never thou didst feel; and wilt desire
> To slink away, and hide thee from His sight:
> And yet wilt have a longing aye to dwell
> Within the Beauty of His countenance.
> And these two pains, so counter and so keen—
> The longing for Him, when thou seest Him not;
> The shame of self at thought of seeing Him,—
> Will be thy veriest, sharpest purgatory.

The wound of love has been used as an image for a high mystical
experience ever since Origen, in his commentary on *The Song of
Songs*, wrote that the soul, 'moved by heavenly love . . . falls

deeply in love with his loveliness and receives from the Word Himself a certain dart and wound of love'; and other Greek Fathers after him, especially Gregory of Nyssa in his commentary on the same Biblical book, have said, like Newman, that this is a healing wound, 'which, by smiting, effects the cure'. Thus here again Newman's language is in the oldest mystical tradition of the Church, and if he places the experience of the 'wound of love' at the meeting of the soul with Christ immediately after death, this is not so far removed from the thought of the Fathers as it might seem, for they place this experience at the end of the mystical life which is also the immediate preparation for the final union of those souls with Christ in heaven that need no further purification.

Newman then describes the pains of purgatory itself, the sharpest of which is the perfect realization of man's unworthiness that is brought about by the vision of Christ, the intense attraction of Christ to whom the soul is longing to go and the awareness of its own unworthiness which keeps it back. This is again paralleled by the final purification of the mystic through the 'dark night of the spirit', the utter desolation, when he is 'yearning' for Christ and yet feels abandoned by him.

The conversation between the soul and its guardian angel is interspersed with hymns sung by choirs of 'Angelicals', explained as 'tender beings . . . least and most childlike of the sons of God', perhaps inspired by the child-angels of the Renaissance painters like Raphael. They accompany the instructions of the guardian angel on the personal destiny of the individual soul with an exposition of the universal destiny of mankind from the creation of Adam, through the fall and the subsequent deterioration of the race, followed by a slow upward development to the triumphant chant of salvation that has become a popular hymn:

> O loving wisdom of our God!
> When all was sin and shame,
> A second Adam to the fight
> And to the rescue came.

This interplay between the personal and the universal, between, as it may perhaps be called, the mystical and the dogmatic elements, is characteristic of Newman, for whom dogmatic and mystical theology were not divided into two different departments, as they had become in modern times, but were inter-related as they had been not only throughout Christian antiquity but still in the thirteenth century, when St Thomas and St Bonaventure were both great systematic and mystical theologians.

As the song of the angelicals dies away the soul approaches the throne of God, now accompanied by the intercession of the Angel of the Agony, who asks Jesus, by the sufferings he has endured for man, to bid the souls come to him. Drawn irresistibly to its Lord, the 'eager spirit' darts from the hold of the guardian angel

> And, with the intemperate energy of love,
> Flies to the dear feet of Emmanuel;
> But, ere it reach them, the keen sanctity,
> Which with its effluence, like a glory, clothes
> And circles round the Crucified, has seized,
> And scorch'd, and shrivell'd it; and now it lies
> Passive and still before the awful Throne.

The soul, now perfectly resigned to its fate, wants only quickly to enter its place of purification, where it is greeted by its fellow sufferers with a beautiful hymn based on the Psalms, especially Psalm 90. Then the guardian angel leaves its charge in purgatory, where 'angels, to whom the willing task is given, shall tend, and nurse and lull' it:

> Farewell, but not for ever! brother dear,
> Be brave and patient on thy bed of sorrow;
> Swiftly shall pass thy night of trial here,
> And I will come and wake thee on the morrow.

Many theologians and mystics have described the sufferings of purgatory as equal to the sufferings of hell, distinguished only by the fact that they will come to an end whereas the torments of hell are eternal. But, like Dante, Newman considers them to be very different; and, unlike even Dante, he thinks that the soul in purgatory is nursed and tended by angels; not for him Dante's 'shades with hollow eyes'. Indeed, even purgatory is described by him more like a mystical state, and hope is its basic characteristic.

I have tried to explain *The Dream of Gerontius* in terms of a mystical experience and as a sort of compendium of Newman's spirituality, nourished on the Fathers, and deeply influenced also by modern thought. I think such an interpretation justified, especially in view of Newman's own remarks in a letter to a priest who wanted him to give still more details: 'You do me too much honour if you think I am to see in a dream everything that is to be seen in the subject dreamed about. I have said what I saw. Various spiritual writers see various aspects of it; and under their protection and pattern I have set down the dream as it came before the sleeper.' By 'dream', Newman surely meant the essence of his spiritual life and teaching. In it was distilled the experience of a man who had lived from his youth in the presence of the 'unseen world', but who had, at the same time, his finger on the pulse of his age, who had thought deeply about the problems of time and eternity, who had realized the emptiness of an existence without God, and whose faith was grounded firmly in the doctrines of the Church, not passively accepted, but truly, 'existentially' lived and assimilated.

In the second half of the year 1865, in which *The Dream of Gerontius* was written, Newman felt that he had to defend the teaching of the Church on the Blessed Virgin Mary against an attack on it by his old friend Pusey in a treatise strangely entitled *Eirenicon* (peace proposal). Here, the patristic influence on Newman's spirituality is even more marked than in *The Dream of Gerontius*. He develops the Mariology of the Church from the theme of the Second Eve, first voiced by Justin Martyr, and the definition of her as Theotokos, Mother of God, at the Council of Ephesus in 431. For, he says: 'The fathers are enough for me. I do not wish to say more than they suggest to me, and will not say less.' In masterly fashion he develops the doctrines of the Church, especially the recently (1854) defined dogma of the Immaculate Conception, from the patristic teaching: 'Have you any intention to deny,' he asks Pusey, 'that Mary was as fully endowed as Eve? Is it any violent inference, that she, who was to co-operate in the redemption of the world, at least was not less endowed with power from on high, than she who, given as a helpmate to her husband, did in the event but co-operate with him for its ruin? If Eve was raised above human nature by that indwelling moral gift which we call grace, is it rash to say that Mary had even a greater grace? . . . And if Eve had this supernatural inward gift given her from the first moment of her personal existence, is it possible to deny that Mary too had this gift from the very first moment of her personal existence? I do not know how to resist this inference: well, this is simply and literally the doctrine of the Immaculate Conception . . . and it really does seem to me bound up in the doctrine of the Fathers, that Mary is the second Eve.'

But Pusey was not only, or even mainly, concerned with doctrine, but with the exaggerations he found in sermons and treatises on the Blessed Virgin, which contained statements like these: 'that the mercy of Mary is infinite; that God has resigned into her hands His omnipotence; that it is safer to seek her than to seek her Son; that the Blessed Virgin is superior to God; that our Lord is subject to her command; that his present disposition towards sinners, as well as His Father's, is to reject them, while the Blessed Mary takes His place as an Advocate with the Father and Son. . . .'

Newman was horrified at such statements, of which he says that 'they seem to me like a bad dream. I could not have conceived them to be said . . . they do but scare and confuse me.' The only explanation he had for them was that they might be 'sayings of Saints in ecstasy'. This, however, they were not, for they are all to be found in treatises on the Blessed Virgin written 'in cold blood' as it were, for example in Alfonsus Liguori's *Glories of Mary*, in Grignion de Montfort's *True Devotion to the Blessed Virgin* and in a host of medieval and later sermons. Newman consoled himself with the idea that these were foreign, not English habits of devotion; one wonders what he would have said had he been told that some of the incriminated statements, including the idea that it is safer to seek Mary than to seek her Son, are to be found in none other than the good medieval Anglo-Saxon Eadmer (*c*.1055-*c*.1123). But Newman's spirituality was built on the Greek and Latin Fathers, he knew hardly anything about the middle ages, and he was, it seems, somewhat frightened of the mystics whom he did not think he could understand—his copy of St John of the Cross for example remained uncut. This fear of mysticism, or, to put it more mildly, the idea that mysticism was not for him, was undoubtedly due to the debased idea of mysticism current in the nineteenth century, when it was identified with strange phenomena, so that it would not have occurred to Newman that many of his beloved Fathers, Origen, Gregory of Nyssa, St Augustine, were themselves mystics of a high order. But how he would have agreed with St John of the Cross that faith is *the* foundation of the interior life, and that even the highest mystical experience, the perfect union with God, still takes place in the sphere of faith, which is so much more important than any visions or other strange phenomena.

It is not surprising that Newman's answer to Pusey met with a somewhat mixed reception: the 'old Catholics', whose spirituality (nourished on such popular prayer books as *The Garden of the Soul*) was very sober, welcomed it, while the converts of the type of Faber and Manning criticized it. Nevertheless, together with the *Apologia* and *The Dream of Gerontius*, the Letter to Pusey re-established Newman's influence to such an extent that he was invited by the Pope to assist at the forthcoming Vatican Council as a theologian.

9 TAKING STOCK OF THE FOUNDATIONS

NEWMAN, however, declined the invitation to the Vatican Council. He elaborated his reasons in a letter to his old friend Mary Giberne, now Sister Maria Pia of the Order of the Visitation, who had been disappointed that he had not accepted the honour: 'I am more happy as I am, than in any other way' he wrote to her. 'I can't bear the kind of trouble which I should have, if I were brought forward in any public way. Recollect, I could not be *in* the Council, unless I were a Bishop—and really and truly I am *not* a theologian. A theologian is one who has mastered theology—who can say how many opinions there are on every point, what authors have taken which, and which is the best—who can discriminate exactly between proposition and proposition, argument and argument, who can pronounce which are safe, which allowable, which dangerous—who can trace the history of doctrines in successive centuries, and apply the principle of former times to the conditions of the present. This it is to be a theologian —this and a hundred things besides—which I am not, and never shall be. Like St Gregory Nazianzen, I like going my own way, and having my time my own, living without pomp or state, or pressing engagements. Put me into official garb, and I am worth nothing; leave me to myself, and every now and then I shall do something.'

Of course, his description of a theologian in this passage is heavily ironical, and his refusal to be called a theologian applies only to this description, for he goes on to compare himself with Gregory of Nazianzus—and this Gregory is just the one Greek Father whose distinctive title is 'the Theologian'! But because in the nineteenth-century theology was at a low ebb in Rome and only those theologians found favour there who were good at the no doubt necessary, but quite uninspired tasks of reducing theology to propositions and distinguishing between them, Newman declined to be called a theologian or to take part in the deliberations preceding and accompanying Vatican I.

He was dismayed when, on March 6, 1870, the definition of papal infallibility was put on the agenda of the Council. This question had been agitated for some time, the foremost English defenders of infallibility being Manning and Ward. Newman opposed such a definition, not because he did not accept the infallibility of the Pope when proclaiming a dogma after due consultation with the bishops of the Church, but because he considered the question not sufficiently thought out and because he feared also that a definition as visualized by the Ward-Manning party would go much too far. A few weeks before the definition, on June 27, Newman wrote: 'I certainly think this agitation of the Pope's Infallibility most unfortunate and ill-advised, and I shall think so even if the Council decrees it, unless I am obliged to believe that the Holy Ghost protects the Fathers from all inexpedient acts (which I do not see is anywhere promised) as well as guides them into all the truth, as He certainly does. There are truths which are inexpedient.'

It is characteristic of Newman's spirituality that despite his strong emphasis on obedience he reserved a large place for individual reason. In the event he submitted at once to the definition—which was in any case very much milder and more circumscribed than the 'Ultramontanes' like Ward and Manning had envisaged. But he did not approve of the manner in which it was done. The final votes were taken on July 18 to the accompaniment of a violent thunderstorm, which no doubt reminded the more bigoted supporters of papal infallibility of the events at Mount Sinai at the giving of the Law. While agreeing that the definition said nothing about the Pope that Newman himself had not always held, he found it 'impossible to deny that it was done with an imperiousness and overbearing wilfulness, which had been a great scandal—

and I cannot think thunder and lightning a mark of approbation, as some persons wish to make out, and the sudden destruction of the Pope's temporal power does not seem a sign of approval either. It suggests too the thought, that to be at once infallible in religion and a despot in temporals, is perhaps too great for mortal man. Very likely there will be some reaction for a time in his favour, but not permanently. . . .' And in another letter on the same subject he wrote: 'There will be surely, sooner or later, an energetic and stern Nemesis for imperious acts, such as now afflict us.'

Here, as in many other respects, Newman's foresight was almost uncanny—unless it should be called prophetic; and perhaps he belongs indeed to the 'prophetic element' in the Church as opposed to the hierarchical. For after the definition of 1870 the Roman authorities became indeed ever more 'imperious' and 'overbearing', and the confusions of our own time may surely be called 'a stern Nemesis'.

For Newman was jealous of 'the glorious liberty of the children of God'. He had just written a book in which he laid the intellectual foundations of the faith as they presented themselves to him, and he saw them in a very different light from that of the Schoolmen and the traditional proofs of the existence of God. It is not the purpose of this book to analyse Newman's philosophical thought, which would in any case be quite beyond the capacities of the present author, but we must at least try to draw out the spiritual implications of *An Essay in Aid of a Grammar of Assent,* perhaps Newman's most mature and most personal work.

There is one straight line that runs from the decisive spiritual experience of the boy of fifteen to the great work of the almost seventy-year-old Christian thinker, and this is the consciousness of God and himself as the two 'absolute and luminously self evident beings'. For Newman it is not the cosmos that first speaks to him of God, but his own conscience: 'From the recurring instances in which conscience acts, forcing upon us importunately the mandate of a Superior, we have fresh and fresh evidence of the existence of a Sovereign Ruler.' He later elaborates this awareness of God through conscience in a way that reflects a most intimate experience: 'If, as is the case, we feel responsibility, are ashamed, are frightened, at transgressing the voice of conscience, this implies that there is One whose claims upon us we fear. If, on doing wrong, we feel the same tearful, broken-hearted sorrow which overwhelms us on hurting a mother; if, on doing right, we enjoy the same serenity of mind, the same soothing, satisfactory delight which follows on our receiving praise from a father, we certainly have within us the image of some person, to whom our love and veneration look, in whose smile we find our happiness, for whom we yearn, towards whom we direct our pleadings, in whose anger we are troubled and waste away.'

For Newman, religion does not begin with a first cause inferred from the world around us but with a Person directly addressing his conscience, and in this he is much nearer to modern thinkers like Pascal, whom he quotes, and his contemporary Kierkegaard, who was unknown to him, than to the Schoolmen and their successors. This Person may impress himself already on the child, and there is certainly again a strong autobiographical element in his description of the child who possesses 'an image of the good God, good in Himself, good relatively to the child, with whatever incompleteness; an image before it has been reflected on, and before it is recognized by him as a notion. . . . Though he cannot explain or define the word "God" . . . his acts show that to him it is far more than a word . . . he has that within him which actually vibrates, responds, and gives a deep meaning to the lessons of his first teachers about the will and the providence of God.'

Philosophical concepts of God such 'first Cause' or 'pure Act' were completely foreign to Newman, for whom God could only be a Person who was apprehended by personal response. Hence his thought about God was never detached, but always involved his whole being, which even from childhood 'vibrates' and 'responds' and finally achieves a union with Him that can only be called mystical, for this is how Newman describes the relation between God and his faithful: 'When men begin all their works with the thought of God, acting for His sake and to fulfil His will, when they ask His blessing on themselves and their life, pray to Him for the objects they desire, and see Him in the event, whether it be according to their prayers or not, they will find everything that happens tend to confirm them in the truths about Him which live in their imagination, varied and unearthly as those truths may be. Then they are brought into His presence as that of a Living Person, and are able to hold converse with Him, and that with a directness and simplicity, with a confidence and intimacy, *mutatis mutandis*, which we use towards an earthly superior; so that it is doubtful whether we realize the company of our fellow-men with greater keenness than these favoured minds are able to contemplate and adore the Unseen, Incomprehensible Creator.'

A man who had not himself experienced a perfect union with God would hardly have introduced such passages in a treatise dealing mainly with the problem of knowledge and the nature of belief. But for Newman God was such an inescapable presence, such a constantly experienced Reality, that he could not write about him in an objective way as if he were a subject among others. To him God was not something or even someone outside (let alone 'up there' or 'out there'), he was a Person with him and in him, for he had 'a sense of the presence of a Supreme Being, which never has been dimmed by even a passing shadow, which had inhabited us ever since we can recollect anything, and which we cannot imagine our losing.'

This intense awareness of the divine presence was quite compatible with an equal intellectual awareness of the difficulties of faith which have always existed, but which have been considerably intensified in modern times. Newman enumerates the existence of evil and suffering, he asks why we are created without our consent, how it is possible that the Supreme Being has no beginning, how his justice can be combined with his love, and how man's behaviour in time can be responsible for his destiny in eternity. 'These, and a host of like questions,' he says, 'must arise in every thoughtful mind.' How can we deal with them without thereby destroying our faith and our whole spiritual life? Newman answers that these are questions which admit of no solution, the human mind simply cannot cope with them. The only way of treating them is to disregard them: 'After the best use of reason [they] must be deliberately put aside, as beyond reason', for they will only 'hinder the direct course of religious inquiry from reaching its destination'. There simply are no cut and dried answers to these ultimate questions which must remain mysteries to the limited human reason, to be accepted as such and to be placed outside the field of enquiry. They will in no way impair the faith of the believer, for 'even what in some minds seems like an undercurrent of scepticism, or a faith founded on a perilous substratum of doubt, need not be more than a temptation, though robbing certitude of its normal peacefulness. In such a case, faith may still express the steady conviction of the intellect, it may still be the grave, deep, calm, prudent assurance of mature experience, though it is not the ready and impetuous assent of the young, the generous, or the unreflecting.'

Newman realized that neither the existence of God nor any other religious truths could be proved in the same way as mathematical propositions. And this, he argues, does not apply only to religious truths, it applies also to most of the facts we accept with complete certitude in our daily life, such as that Britain is an island or that America lies to the west of it, though we have neither mathematical proof of it nor the direct evidence of our senses. What makes us sure of these facts is a number of converging probabilities; it is the same with the religious truths which we accept. These themselves are not merely probable, but what leads us to accept them as certain is a number of probabilities. We are as certain of them as we are of any proposition resting on cogent logical proof—but the way by which we arrive at these truths is different.

By basing Christian belief and with it the spiritual life on the evidence of conscience on the one hand and on the acceptance of converging probabilities on the other, Newman freed them from the straitjacket of logic used in the theological textbooks which he held to be incapable of dealing with *facts*, and assigned them to the province of what he calls the *illative sense*, which may roughly be explained as the faculty in us which enables us to reach conclusions which are certain without the apparatus of syllogisms. This 'illative sense', which in its perfection is very near to what is called 'intuition', is the faculty by which we apprehend religious truths. It seems to the present writer also to be an excellent explanation of contemplative prayer, when the mind does not, as in meditation, proceed in orderly fashion from one subject to another but apprehends its object as it were in one comprehensive glance— a form of prayer which Newman had certainly practised himself for a long time, as he had written already during his Advent Retreat of 1843: 'I do not know what has come to me—I seem to have less and less matter, and less and less to think about.'

Newman certainly used his own experience and his own 'illative sense' to build up evidence for religious faith and he anticipated that this would be held against the possibility of a general acceptance of his argumentation. 'Of course,' he wrote, 'I cannot hope to carry all inquiring minds with me . . . I have appealed to the testimony given implicitly by our conscience to the Divine Being and His Attributes, and there are those, I know, whose experience will not respond to the appeal—doubtless; but are there any truths which have reality, whether of experience or of reason, which are not disputed by some schools of philosophy or some bodies of men?'

Newman was, and sometimes still is, attacked for basing his evidence for the existence of God and the truth of Christianity on personal experience. This is true in the sense that his own experience gave him the impulse to seek for a way of making these doctrines more easily accessible to his contemporaries than the old scholastic proofs. It is most emphatically not true in the sense that he equated religious truth with personal experience. For him the doctrines of the Church were objective reality, but the way in which men accepted them was the way of personal apprehension of their truth, not the way of following syllogisms.

The intensity of Newman's spirituality shows itself most impressively in what he says about the acceptance of dogma and the 'real' as opposed to the merely 'notional assent' to it. 'What an illustration of the real assent which can be given to this proposition [viz. "The Son is God"], and its power over our affections and emotions, is the first half of the first Chapter of St John's Gospel or again the vision of our Lord in the first chapter of the Apocalypse! or the first chapter of St John's first Epistle! Again, how burning are St Paul's words when he speaks of our Lord's crucifixion and death! What is the secret of that flame, but this same dogmatic sentence, "The Son is God"? . . . This same power of the dogma may be illustrated from the Ritual. Consider the services for Christmas or Epiphany; for Easter, Ascension, and (I may say) pre-eminently Corpus Christi; what are these great Festivals but comments on the words, "The Son of God"? Yet who will say that they have the subtlety, the aridity, the coldness of mere scholastic science? Are they addressed to the pure intellect, or to the imagination? do they interest our logical faculty, or excite our devotion? Why is it that personally we often find ourselves so ill-fitted to take part in them, except that we are not good enough, that in our case the dogma is far too much a theological notion, far too little an image living within us?'

For to Newman dogma is a living reality, and it is significant that the so-called Athanasian Creed, also called the *Quicunque,* was his favourite hymn. Just this Creed is considered by many of our contemporaries to be quite antiquated and with its precise theological explanations and the condemnation of those who will not accept them as an example of the dry theology and the narrow-minded dogmatism of the Church. For Newman it was the apogee of the faith: 'It is not a mere collection of notions,' he writes, 'however momentous. It is a psalm or hymn of praise, of confession, and of profound, self-prostrating homage, parallel to the canticles of the elect in the Apocalypse. It appeals to the imagination quite as much as to the intellect. It is the war-song of faith, with which we warn first ourselves, then each other, and then all those who are within its hearing, and the hearing of the Truth, who our God is, and how we must worship Him, and how vast our responsibility will be if we know what to believe, and yet believe not. . . . For myself I have ever felt it as the most simple and sublime, the most devotional formulary to which Christianity has given birth, more so even than the *Veni Creator* and the *Te Deum*. Even the antithetical form of its sentences, which is a stumbling-block to so many, as seeming to force, and to exult in forcing a mystery upon recalcitrating minds, has to my apprehension . . . a very different drift. It is intended as a check upon our reasonings, lest they rush on in one direction beyond the limits of the truth, and it turns them back into the opposite direction. Certainly it implies a glorying in the Mystery; but it is not simply a statement of the Mystery for the sake of its mysteriousness.'

So in this, Newman's last great work in which he summed up his most intimate thought and experience, we find even more than in *The Dream of Gerontius* the strong patristic influence combined with the modern 'existential' attitude to theology. He glories in the subtleties of the thought of the Greek Fathers who proclaimed the three Persons in the one Nature of the Godhead and the two Natures in the one Person of the incarnate Christ in the thundering antitheses of the *Quicunque*, and he brings his own subtlety to bear on the way in which this mysterious Creed is accepted and lived by modern man. For the *Essay in Aid of a Grammar of Assent*, as Newman modestly called his book, shows perhaps more clearly than any of his other works how deeply his faith was rooted in the tradition of the Church while he was nevertheless intensely conscious of all the difficulties modern men had to face in accepting this tradition. In this Newman was, indeed, like the scribe trained for the kingdom of heaven, 'who brings out of his treasure what is new and what is old'.

The 'new', however, was too new for some of his contemporaries, who criticized it because Newman's way of presenting Christianity did not fit into the scholastic categories, though others including Ward, welcomed the book as a most useful weapon to combat the unbelief of the times. Newman himself had achieved the serenity that made him indifferent to blame: 'I have done my best, and given my all, and I leave it to Him to prosper or not, as He thinks fit, for Whom I have done it.' Besides, he had found that ideas which had been thought daring at the time he had first expressed them were later accepted as perfectly orthodox, as had happened to his *Essay on Development*, so 'as I waited patiently as regards my former work [on Development], for "Time to be the Father of Truth", so now I leave the judgement between Fr Harper [who had attacked the Grammar] and me to the sure future.'

Thus Newman had reached perfect detachment from the opinions of the world, but not detachment in the sense of being unfeeling. For just these years after the publication of the *Essay* and the Vatican Council were a time of deep sorrow, as one of his friends after the other died, the greatest loss of all being Ambrose St John, who died in 1875. So he wrote to the Duchess of Norfolk, 'I too am like a tree stripped of its greenness and strength in losing first one and then another of my dearest friends'. But beside the natural sorrow there was the supernatural hope, so that, in 1880, he could say: 'Looking beyond this life, my first prayer, aim, and hope is that I may see God. The thought of being blest with the sight of earthly friends pales before that thought. I believe that I shall never die; this awful prospect would crush me, were it not that I trusted and prayed that it would be an eternity in God's Presence.'

By then the cloud that had been hanging over him, the mistrust of the authorities, had been 'lifted for ever'; for in May 1879, when he was seventy-eight years of age, the new Pope, Leo XIII, had made him a Cardinal, thus setting the seal of approval by the highest authority on his life's work.

As we have tried to follow both Newman's own spiritual development and his teaching, what is perhaps one of their most striking features is how his early prayer to be preserved from being made proud by success was answered throughout his life. When he was at the peak of his influence in Oxford, he had to leave the Church of England and become a Catholic; and as soon as he had established a certain position in the Church of Rome, he became suspect to the authorities and felt himself 'under a cloud'. Time and again he was aware that his work would never be fully understood or recognized by his contemporaries, and his greatest cross was that he realized so clearsightedly the needs of his time, the necessity of freeing religion from those inessential accretions of past centuries that were unacceptable to modern men and of establishing a 'dialogue', to use a modern catchword, with contemporary thought, and that just this very clearsightedness made him suspect. At the very end of his life the cloud lifted; but after his death (1890) at the beginning of this century, his principles were once more rejected, and after the Modernist controversy the clock was put back again and free discussion stifled until the windows were opened to the outside world and the siege mentality began to give way in our own time.

By now the spirit of Newman has penetrated many departments of Christian thought, but spirituality seems to have lagged behind. True, he never wrote a treatise on spirituality, indeed, he thought himself incompetent in this sphere, which Faber and Dalgairns had arrogated to themselves. Yet, as I hope to have shown in the preceding pages, Newman's whole life and all his teaching were shot through with the intense awareness of God and the 'unseen world'; he himself led a deeply spiritual life, and both his sermons and most of his other works are saturated with spiritual teaching, a teaching that is based on Scripture and the Fathers and is at the same time wide open to the problems of the modern world. It is, moreover, a teaching that embraces the whole man, not only 'souls', and that penetrates the whole human life.

It can hardly be denied that our spirituality suffers from a surfeit of departmentalization. Without realizing it, Newman re-integrated it with philosophy and theology, or rather he made it the source that enlivened both because it was the centre and the foundation of his own life. In this, as in so much else, he is a safe guide to be followed by modern Christians who must recover that sense of the 'unseen world' of which Newman was so intensely aware, if they are once more to become a leaven in our unbelieving and materialistic world.

APPENDIX

Newman on Lives of the Saints

(Introductory to his Essay on St Chrysostom, first published in the Rambler *of 1859-60 and republished in volume II of his Historical Sketches)*

I CONFESS to a delight in reading the lives, and dwelling on the characters and actions, of the Saints of the first ages, such as I receive from none besides them; and for this reason, because we know so much more about them than about most of the Saints who come after them. People are variously constituted; what influences one does not influence another. There are persons of warm imaginations, who can easily picture to themselves what they never saw. They can at will see Angels and Saints hovering over them when they are in church; they see their lineaments, their features, their motions, their gestures, their smile or their grief. They can go home and draw what they have seen, from the vivid memory of what, while it lasted, was so transporting. I am not one of such; I am touched by my five senses, by what my eyes behold and my ears hear. I am touched by what I read about, not by what I myself create. As faith need not lead to practice, so in me mere imagination does not lead to devotion. I gain more from the life of our Lord in the Gospels than from a treatise *de Deo*.* I gain more from three verses of St John than from the three points of a meditation. I like a Spanish crucifix of painted wood more than one from Italy, which is made of gold. I am more touched by the Seven Dolours† than by the Immaculate Conception; I am more

* Treatise on God in traditional Roman Catholic manuals.
† Traditional seven sorrows of the Blessed Virgin.

devout to St Gabriel than to one of Isaiah's seraphim. I love St Paul
more than one of those first Carmelites, his contemporaries, whose
names and acts no one ever heard of; I feel affectionately towards
the Alexandrian Dionysius, I do homage to St George. I do not
say that my way is better than another's; but it is my way, and an
allowable way. And it is the reason why I am so specially attached
to the Saints of the third and fourth century, because we know so
much about them. This is why I feel a devout affection for St
Chrysostom. He and the rest of them have written autobiography
on a large scale; they have given us their own histories, their
thoughts, words, and actions, in a number of goodly folios, pro-
ductions which are in themselves some of their meritorious
works.

   I do not know where else to find the daily life, the secret heart,
of such favoured servants of God, unveiled to their devout disciples
in such completeness and fidelity. Modern times afford some
instances of the kind : St Theresa is one of them; St Francis de
Sales is another : still, on the whole, what should we have known
of the generality of the great Saints of the later centuries, had we
been left to themselves for the information? We should of course
have had the treasure of their recorded visions, prophecies, and
meditations; but these are portions of their divine, not their human
life, and rather belong to what God did for them, than to what
they did for themselves. There is one circumstance, indeed, which
tells in their favour; we have their portraits. This, I grant, is in
favour of the moderns; certainly we have no idea at all of the
personal appearance, the expression of countenance, or the bearing
of St Athanasius or St Hilary. It is assuredly a great point, if the
case be so, that we have likenesses of the modern Saints. But I am
not sure that we have; often there was no attempt at all made to
take their likenesses in their lifetime; sometimes they would not
let themselves be taken when there was. St Philip Neri once caught
an artist in the very commission of that great offence, and stopped
him; and the unfinished picture hangs up to this day at the *Pelle-
grini*, a memorial of a painter's devotion and a saint's modesty.
Sometimes, again, there may be a good likeness; but, perhaps,

however interesting in itself, it was taken before the Saint's conversion, and can only satisfy a human curiosity: sometimes it was taken, indeed, but has been lost, and the copies, if there are any, are not to be trusted. Sometimes the artist's veneration has idealized the countenance, or the popular demand has vulgarized it. How has a devout poetry embellished some of the ordinary portraits of the great St Carlo!* how does the original likeness of St Ignatius differ from the military countenance and figure which ordinary pencils have bestowed upon him! You cannot thus wander from the original, in the new edition you put to press of St Ambrose or the blessed Theodoret.

I repeat, what I want to trace and study is the real, hidden but human, life, or the *interior*, as it is called, of such glorious creations of God; and this I gain with difficulty from mere biographies. Those biographies are most valuable both as being true and as being edifying; they are true to the letter, as far as they record facts and acts; I know it: but actions are not enough for sanctity; we must have saintly motives; and as to these motives, the actions themselves seldom carry the motives along with them. In consequence, they are often supplied simply by the biographer out of his own head; and with good reason supplied, from the certainty which he feels that, since it is the act of a Saint which he is describing, therefore it must be a saintly act. Properly and naturally supplied, I grant: but I can do that as well as he; and ought to do it for myself, and shall be sure to do it, if I make the Saint my meditation. The biographer in that case is no longer a mere witness and reporter; he has become a commentator. He gives me no insight into the Saint's *interior*; he does but tell me to infer that the Saint acted in some transcendent way from the reason of the case, or to hold it on faith because he has been canonized. For instance: When I read in such a life, 'The Saint, when asked a question, was silent from humility', or 'from compassion for the ignorance of the speaker', or 'in order to give him a gentle rebuke'—I find a motive assigned, whichever of the three is selected, which is the biographer's own, and perhaps has two chances to one against its

* St Charles Borromeo.

being the right one. We read of an occasion on which St Athanasius said nothing, but smiled, when a question was put to him: it was another Saint who asked the question, and who has recorded the smile; but he does not more than doubtfully explain it. Many a biographer would, simply out of piety, have pronounced the reason of that smile. I should not blame him for doing so; but it was more than he could do as a biographer; if he did it, he would do it, not as an historian, but as a spiritual writer.

On the other hand, when a Saint is himself the speaker, he interprets his own action; and that is what I find done in such fulness in the case of those early luminaries of the Church to whom I am referring. I want to hear a Saint converse; I am not content to look at him as a statue; his words are the index of his hidden life, as far as that life can be known to man, for 'out of the abundance of the heart the mouth speaketh'. This is why I exult in the folios of the Fathers. I am not obliged to read the whole of them, I read what I can and am content. Though I may not have advanced into their *interior* more than a certain way, still, what I have read is good so far as it goes. It does not derogate from the reality of that knowledge and love of a Saint which I have actually got from what I have read already of his writings, that there is much more of those writings to be read and much more of him to be loved. Cannot we know and love the King of Saints? Yet we ever can know more and more about Him, and gain further motives for loving Him.

Now the Ancient Saints have left behind them just that kind of literature which more than any other represents the abundance of the heart, which more than any other approaches to conversation; I mean correspondence. Why is it that we feel an interest in Cicero which we cannot feel in Demosthenes or Plato? Plato is the very type of soaring philosophy, and Demosthenes of forcible eloquence; Cicero is something more than orator and a sage; he is not a mere ideality, he is a man and a brother; he is one of ourselves. We do not merely believe it, or infer it, but we have the enduring and living evidence of it—how? In his letters. He can be

studied, criticized if you will; but still dwelt upon and sympath-
ized with also. Now the case of the Ancient Saints is parallel to that
of Cicero. We have their letters in a marvellous profusion. We have
above 400 letters of St Basil's; above 200 of St Augustine's. St
Chrysostom has left us about 240; St Gregory Nazianzen the same
number; Pope St Gregory as many as 840. St Nilus close on 1400
short ones; St Isidore, 1440.* The blessed Theodoret, 146; St Leo,
140; St Cyprian, 80 or 90; St Paulinus, 50; St Jerome, above 100;
St Ambrose, 90. St Bernard, the last of the fathers, supplies 444;
and St Anselm, the first of the schoolmen, nearly the same number. I am passing beyond the early Saints; so I might go on to
certain modern, as St Francis Xavier; but they all belong to one
school of literature, which is now well-nigh extinct.

These letters are of very various characters, compared one with
another: a large portion of them were intended simply for the
parties to whom they are addressed; a large portion consist of brief
answers to questions asked of the writer, or a few words of good
counsel or spiritual exhortation, disclosing his character either by
the topic selected, or his mode of dealing with it. Many are doctrinal; great numbers, again, are strictly ecclesiastical and *ex
cathedrâ*. Many are historical and biographical; some might be
called state-papers; some narrate public transactions, and how the
writer felt towards them, or why he took part in them. Pope
Gregory's epistles give us the same sort of insight into the holy
solicitude for the universal Christian people which possessed him,
that minute vigilance, yet comprehensive superintendence of the
chief pastor, which in a very different field of labour is seen in the
Duke of Wellington's despatches on campaign, which tell us so
much more about him than any panegyrical sketch. Those of St
Isidore and St Nilus consist of little more than one or two terse,
pithy, pregnant sentences, which may be called sermonets, and
are often as vivid as if we heard them. St Chrysostom's are for the
most part crowded into the three memorable years in which the
sufferings of exile gradually ripened into a virtual martyrdom.
Others, as some of those of St Jerome and St Ambrose, are medi-

---

* These Letters are not all authentic.

tations on mystical subjects. Those of St Dionysius of Alexandria, which are but fragments, recount the various trials of the time, and are marked with a vigorous individuality which invests the narrative with an interest far higher than historical.

This manifestation of themselves the Ancient Saints carry with them into other kinds of composition, where it was less to be expected. Instead of writing formal doctrinal treatises, they write controversy; and their controversy, again, is correspondence. They mix up their own persons, natural and supernatural, with the didactic or polemical works which engaged them. Their authoritative declarations are written, not on stone tablets, but on what Scripture calls 'the fleshy tables of the heart'. The line of their discussion traverses a region rich and interesting, and opens on those who follow them in it a succession of instructive views as to the aims, the difficulties, the disappointments, under which they journeyed on heavenward, their care of the brethren, their anxieties about contemporary teachers of error. Dogma and proof are in them at the same time hagiography. They do not write a *summa theologiae*,* or draw out a *catena*,† or pursue a single thesis through the stages of a scholastic disputation. They wrote for the occasion, and seldom on a carefully-digested plan.

The same remark holds of their comments upon Scripture. A speaker and an audience are prominent throughout them; and we gain an insight into their own character and the circumstances of their times, while we are indoctrinated in the sacred text. When Pope Gregory comments upon Ezechiel, he writes about the Lombards, his own people, and himself. What a vivid idea we have of St Chrysostom! partly from his style, partly from his matter; yet we gain it from his formal expositions of Scripture. His expositions are discourses; his discourses, whether he will or no, are manifestations. St Gregory Nazianzen has written discourses too, by means of which he has gained for himself the special title of 'Theologus'; yet these same orations give us also a large range of

---

* *Summa theologiae*, treatise covering the whole field of Catholic doctrine; the most celebrated is that of St Thomas Aquinas.

† Latin *catena* = chain, string of explanation of scriptural texts by various authors.

information about his own life, his kindred and friends, his feelings and his fortunes; and, as if this were not enough, he has bequeathed to us, besides his letters, his poems, a huge collection of miscellaneous verse, full of himself and his times. They are his confessions.

Here I am reminded of the celebrated work of St Augustine's which bears that name, and which has no parallel in sacred literature. Of the same character are portions of the correspondence of St Basil, and, again, of St Jerome. It is remarkable, on the other hand, that certain ancient writers, who, able and learned as they are, have no title to be called Saints such as Tertullian and Eusebius, afford as few instances as possible in their works, as far as I know, of that tenderness and simiplicity of character which leads their saintly contemporaries to an unstudied self-manifestation.

It is perhaps presumptuous in me to have spoken of the Fathers thus universally, and I may have made mistakes in detail; but I have confidence in my general principle, and its general exemplification in their case. Words are the exponents of thoughts, and a silent Saint is the object of faith rather than of affection. If he speaks, then we have the original before us; if he is silent, we must put up with a copy, done with more or less skill according to the painter. But in saying this, I do not mark off the Saints into two distinct classes, those who speak and those who are silent; I am only contrasting two kinds of exhibition which are variously fulfilled in them, taken one by one. Nor is a silent Saint one who does not write, but one who does not speak; and some of them may manifest themselves by their short sayings and their single words more graphically than if they had written a volume. When St Philip Neri excused his abstemiousness on the ground of his fear lest he should get as fat as his friend Francesco Scarletti, or hid his religious tears with the jest, 'Mayn't a poor orphan weep, who has neither father nor mother?' or made Consolini read out loud a story-book to him, when certain great lords of Poland came to see a Saint, he let us into his character better than by many treatises.

Nor are any words at all necessary in some cases; for I suppose the Martyrs, who are the most ancient Saints of all, speak by their deaths; whereas some of the Fathers, as St Isidore of Seville, and various medieval Saints, have written many large books, and tell us, alas! about themselves nothing. And further still, in the present state of education among us, I do not see how it is possible we should enjoy that personal knowledge of the Saints which seems to me so desirable. The bulk of the faithful have nothing at all to do with Saints' lives or writings, for this simple reason, because they cannot read, or do not like reading. They are devout to a Saint, as they are devout to their Guardian Angel, because he is a work of God, full of grace and glory, and able to protect them. I recollect an Irishman of the humblest class complaining of the sermon of a Religious because it had nothing in it about the Saints: the fact was not so at all, and in the pulpit from which the sermon was preached there had been much about Saints Sunday after Sunday. But it turned out that the complainant was devout to St Joseph; and his real grievance was, that St Joseph was not mentioned in the sermon. Nor did he want more than the mention of his glorious patron's name; his very name inspired devotion, he needed no life of him. I wish we, with all our learning, were sure of having this poor man's devotion; but that wish is nothing to the purpose in my present argument, in which I am not contrasting educated and uneducated piety, but the popular biographies of Saints and their actual writings.

Nor must it be supposed that I think lightly of the debt of gratitude which we owe to their biographers. It is not their fault if their Saint has been silent; all that we know about him, be it much, be it little, we owe to them. As I was saying just now, some of those saints who have written most have told us least. There is St Thomas; he was called in his youth the Bos Siculus* for his silence; it is one of the few personal traits which we have of him, and for that very reason, though it does but record the privation of which I am complaining, it is worth a good deal. It is a great consolation to know that he was the Bos Siculus; it makes us feel a sympathy

---

* Eng. 'dumb ox', nickname given to St Thomas Aquinas.

with him, and leads us to trust that perhaps he will feel some sympathy for us, who for one reason or other are silent at times when we should like to be speaking. But it is the sole consolation for that forlorn silence of his, since, although at length he broke it to some purpose, as regards theology, and became a marvel (according to the proverb in such cases), still he is as silent as before in regard to himself. The Angel of the schools! how overflowing he must have been, I say to myself, in all bright supernatural visions, and beautiful and sublime thoughts! how serene in his contemplation of them! how winning in his communication! but he has not helped me ever so little in apprehending what I firmly believe about him. He wrote his *Summa* and his *Hymns* under obedience, I suppose; and no obedience was given him to speak of himself. So we are thrown upon his biographers, and but for them, we should speak of him as we speak of the author of the *Imitation* or of the *Veni Creator*, only as of a great unknown benefactor. All honour, then, and gratitude to the writers of Saints' lives. They have done what they could. It would not have improved matters if they had been silent as well as the Saint; still they cannot make up for their Saint's silence; they do not deprive me of my grievance, that at present I do not really know those to whom I am devout, whom I hope to see in heaven.

A Saint's writings are to me his real 'Life'; and what *is called* his 'Life' is not the outline of an individual, but either of the *auto-saint* or of a myth. Perhaps I shall be asked what I mean by 'Life'. I mean a narrative which impresses the reader with the idea of moral unity, identity, growth, continuity, personality. When a Saint converses with me, I am conscious of the presence of one active principle of thought, one individual character, flowing on and into the various matters which he discusses, and the different transactions in which he mixes. It is what no memorials can reach, however skilfully elaborated, however free from effort or study, however conscientiously faithful, however guaranteed by the veracity of the writers. Why cannot art rival the lily or the rose? Because the colours of the flower are developed and blended by

the force of an inward life; while on the other hand, the lights
and shades of the painter are diligently laid on from without. A
magnifying glass will show the difference. Nor will it improve
matters, though not one only, but a dozen good artists successively
take part in the picture; even if the outline is unbroken, the
colouring is muddy. Commonly, what is called 'the Life', is little
more than a collection of anecdotes brought together from a number of independent quarters; anecdotes striking, indeed, and edifying, but valuable in themselves rather than valuable as parts of a
biography; valuable whoever was the subject of them, not valuable
as illustrating a particular Saint. It would be difficult to mistake
for each other a paragraph of St Ambrose, or of St Jerome, or of
St Augustine; it would be very easy to mistake a chapter in the
life of one holy missionary or nun for a chapter in the life of
another.

An almsgiving here, an instance of meekness there, a severity
of penance, a round of religious duties—all these things humble
me, instruct me, improve me; I cannot desire any thing better of
their kind; but they do not necessarily coalesce into the image of
a person. From such works I do but learn to pay devotion to an
abstract and typical perfection under a certain particular name;
I do not know more of the real Saint who bore it than before.
Saints, as other men, differ from each other in this, that the multitude of qualities which they have in common are differently combined in each of them. This forms one great part of their personality. One Saint is remarkable for fortitude; not that he has not
other heroic virtues by *concomitance*, as it may be called, but by
virtue of that one gift in particular he has won his crown. Another
is remarkable for patient hope, another for renunciation of the
world. Such a particular virtue may be said to give form to all the
rest which are grouped round it, and are moulded and modified
by means of it. Thus it is that often what is right in one would be
wrong in another; and, in fact, the very same action is allowed or
chosen by one, and shunned by another, as being consistent or
inconsistent with their respective characters—pretty much as in
the combination of colours, each separate tint takes a shade from

the rest, and is good or bad from its company. The whole gives a meaning to the parts; but it is difficult to rise from the parts to the whole. When I read St Augustine or St Basil, I hold converse with a beautiful grace-illumined soul, looking out into this world of sense, and leavening it with itself; when I read a professed life of him, I am wandering in a labyrinth of which I cannot find the centre and heart, and am but conducted out of doors again when I do my best to penetrate within.

This seems to me, to tell the truth, a sort of pantheistic treatment of the Saints. I ask something more than to stumble upon the *disjecta membra* of what ought to be a living whole. I take but a secondary interest in books which chop up a Saint into chapters of faith, hope, charity, and the cardinal virtues. They are too scientific to be devotional. They have their great utility, but it is not the utility which they profess. They do not manifest a Saint, they mince him into spiritual lessons. They are rightly called spiritual reading, that is just what they are, and they cannot possibly be any thing better; but they are not any thing else. They contain a series of points of meditation on particular virtues, made easier because those points are put under the patronage and the invocation of a Saint. With a view to learning real devotion to him, I prefer (speaking for myself) to have any one action or event of his life drawn out minutely, with his own comments upon it, than a score of virtues, or of acts of one virtue, strung together in as many sentences. Now, in the ancient writings I have spoken of, certain transactions are thoroughly worked out. We know all that happened to a Saint on such or such an occasion, all that was done by him. We have a view of his character, his tastes, his natural infirmities, his struggles and victories over them, which in no other way can be attained. And therefore it is that, without quarelling with the devotion of others, I give the preference to my own.

This is why it is so difficult to be patient with such Church histories as Mosheim's,* putting out of the question his Protestant

* Johann Lorenz von Mosheim (1694-1755), German Protestant theologian, whose Church history had been translated into English in 1841.

N

prejudices. When you have read through a century of him, you have as little distinct idea of what he has been about, as when you began. You have been hurried about from subject to subject, from external history to internal, from ceremonies to divines, from heresies to persecutions, till you find that you have gained nothing but to be fatigued. If history is to mirror the actual course of time, it must also be a course itself; it must not be the mere emptying out of a portfolio of unconnected persons and events, which are not synchronous, nor co-ordinate, nor correlative, but merely arranged, if arrangement it can be called, according to the convenience of the author. And I have a parallel difficulty in the case of hagiographers, when they draw out their materials, not according to years, but according to virtues. Such reading is not history, it is moral science; nay, hardly that : for chronological considerations will be neglected; youth, manhood, and age, will be intermingled. I shall not be able to trace out, for my own edification, the solemn conflict which is waging in the soul between what is divine and what is human, or the eras of the successive victories won by the powers and principles which are divine. I shall not be able to determine whether there was heroism in the young, whether there was not infirmity and temptation in the old. I shall not be able to explain actions which need explanation, for the age of the actors is the true key for entering into them. I shall be wearied and disappointed, and I shall go back with pleasure to the Fathers.

Here another great subject opens upon us, when I ought to be bringing these remarks to an end; I mean the endemic perennial fidget which possesses us about giving scandal; facts are omitted in great histories, or glosses are put upon memorable acts, because they are thought not edifying, whereas of all scandals such omissions, such glosses, are the greatest. But I am getting far more argumentative than I thought to be when I began; so I lay my pen down, and retire into myself.

BIBLIOGRAPHY

I⊤ is a shameful fact that no complete edition of Newman's Works exists in this country and many of his writings are out of print. I shall cite here the most important ones for the present subject. When available, the American editions are cited, when there is no American edition I list the editions I have used.

1. *Letters and Autobiographical Writings*
   Apologia pro Vita Sua, New York, Oxford University Press, 1964.
   Autobiographical Writings, ed. H. Tristram, London, Sheed & Ward, 1956.
   Letters and Correspondence of John Henry Newman, ed. Anne Mozley, 2 vols., London, Longmans, 1898.
   The Letters and Diaries of John Henry Newman, ed. C. Stephen Dessain, vols. 11-17, Westminster, Md., The Newman Press, 1961, 1962, 1963, 1964, 1965.

2. *Sermons*
   Catholic Sermons, London, Burns & Oates, 1957.
   Discourses Addressed to Mixed Congregations, London, Longmans, 1899.
   Parochial and Plain Sermons, 8 vols., London, Rivingtons, 1868; available New York, D. Appleton & Co, 1843.
   Sermons Bearing on Subjects of the Day, London, Longmans, 1898.
   Sermons on Various Occasions, London, Burns & Lambert, 1858.
   Sermons Preached before the University of Oxford, London, Longmans, 1898.

3. *Lectures and Essays*

Certain Difficulties Felt by Anglicans, 2 vols., London, Longmans, 1891-92.

Discussions and Arguments, London, Longmans, 1885.

Essays Critical and Historical, 2 vols., London, Pickering, 1871.

An Essay in Aid of a Grammar of Assent, New York, Longmans, 1947.

An Essay on the Development of Christian Doctrine, New York, Doubleday.

Historical Sketches, 2 vols., London, Longmans, 1917.

The Idea of a University, New York, Holt Rinehart & Winston, 1959.

Lectures on Justification, London, Longmans, 1892.

Lectures on the Present Position of Catholics in England, 4th ed., London, Burns & Oates, 1872.

On Consulting the Faithful on Matters of Doctrine, New York, Sheed & Ward, 1962.

Two Essays on Biblical and Ecclesiastical Miracles, London, Longmans, 1918.

The Via Media of the Anglican Church, 2 vols., London, Longmans, 1908.

4. *Novels*

Callista, London, Westminster, Md., The Newman Press, 1962.

Loss and Gain, London, Burns & Oates, 1962.

5. *Various Writings*

The Arians of the Fourth Century, London, Longmans, 1891.

Meditations and Devotions, Springfield, Ill., Templegate.

Verses on Various Occasions, London, Longmans, 1900. Available in Prose and Poetry selected by G. Tillotson, Cambridge, Mass., Harvard University Press, 1957.

The two authoritative biographies of Newman are:

Wilfrid Ward, *The Life of John Henry Cardinal Newman*, 2 vols., New York, Longmans, Green & Co, 1912.

Meriol Trevor, *Newman*, 2 vols., New York, Doubleday, 1962.

Other writings on Newman:
Louis Bouyer, *Newman*, New York, P. J. Kenedy & Sons, 1958.
F. L. Cross, *Newman*, London, P. Allan, 1933.
C. S. Dessain, *John Henry Newman*, London, Nelson, 1966.
Jean Honoré, *Itinéraire spirituel de Newman*, Paris, Editions du Seuil, 1964.
John Henry Newman, Centenary Essays, London, Burns & Oates, 1945.
J. Lewis May, *Cardinal Newman*, New York, Longmans, Green & Co., 1937.
R. D. Middleton, *Newman at Oxford*, Oxford University Press, 1950.
J. Elliot Ross, *John Henry Newman*, W. W. Norton & Co., 1933.
H. Tristram, *Newman and his Friends*, New York, David McKay, 1946.
Maisie Ward, *Young Mr Newman*, London, Sheed & Ward, 1948.

INDEX OF NAMES

Achilli, G. G., 119, 121, 122-5, 137, 153.

Adam, 66, 167

Aeschylus, 27

Alban Hall, 28

Albert, St, 126

Andrew, St, 123

Angelico, Fra, 164

Antony, St, of Egypt, 164

Aristotle, 27

Arnold, Thomas, 42f

Athanasius, St, 86

Augustine, St, of Hippo, 59, 79, 112, 149, 171

Badeley, E. L., 94

Barberi, see Dominic

Basil, St, of Caesarea, 112

Bellarmin, St Robert, 129

Benedict, St, of Nursia, 112

Bernard, St, of Clairvaux, 73, 126

Bonaventure, St, 168

Bowles, Emily, 145

Bowles, Frederick Sellwood, 93

Burns, James, 105

Calvin, John, see Subject Index s.v. Calvinism

Campbell, J., 124

Chalcedon, Council of, 79

Chrysostom, St John, 27, 111f, 149; see also Appendix

Cicero, 27

Coleridge, John Taylor, 125

Connelly, Cornelia, 145

Conservative Journal, 94

Cross, F. L., 47, 49

Cyril, St, of Alexandria, 149

Dalgairns, J. D., 110, 123, 133, 135ff, 155, 182

Dante, 169

Darnell, Nicholas, 150, 153

Dominic Barberi, 100

Dublin Review, 79, 119, 122

Eadmer, 171

Ephesus, Council of, 139, 169

Esau, 96

Eve, 72, 170

Faber, Frederic William, 9, 107, 110f, 113, 133f, 138, 153f, 159, 171, 182

Flanagan, Stanislas, 150

Francis, St, of Assisi, 69, 128

Freud, Sigmund, 143

Froude, Hurrell, 30f, 36, 40

Garden of the Soul, 171

Gennaro, Italian servant, 40

Gentili, Luigi, 95
Giberne, Mary, 172
Globe, 155
Goethe, J. W., 38
Grant, 43
Gregory XVI, 103
Gregory of Nazianzus, 172
Gregory of Nyssa, 126, 167, 171

Hammond, Henry, 50
Harper, Rev., 181
Harris, Miss, 105
Hawkins, Edward, 25
Hooker, Richard, 50
Hope, J. R., 87
Horace, 27
Hume, David, 12

Ignatius, St, of Antioch, 30
Ignatius, St, of Loyola, 91, 103, 136
Imitation of Christ, 82

Jacob, 96
Januarius, St, 104
Jerome, St, 149
Jesuits, 91
John, St, Evangelist, 15, 70
John XXIII, 144, 149
John, St, of the Cross, 74, 94, 126, 136, 142, 171
Joseph, St, 147
Joshua, 28
Judas, 51
Justin the Martyr, 30, 163, 169

Keble, John, 23, 42, 47, 49, 76, 86f, 101, 151
Ken, Thomas, 50

Kierkegaard, Søren, 68, 84, 162, 175
Kingsley, Charles, 157
Kretschmer, Ernst, 35

Laud, William, 31
Lazarus, 52
Leo XIII, 181
Liguori, St Alfonsus, 170
Lincolnshire Express, 155
Lockhart, Martha, 103
Lockhart, William, 95
Longmans, publishers, 125
Luther, *see* Lutheranism in Subject Index

Macmillan's Magazine, 157
Manning, Henry Edward, 157, 171, 173
Mary, the Blessed Virgin, *see* Subject Index
Mayers, Walter, 13, 15, 18, 24, 30
Merton, Thomas, 129
Montfort, St Grignion de, 170
More, St Thomas, 149
Mozley, Anne, 82
Mozley, Harriet, Newman's eldest sister, 16, 23, 38, 98
Mozley, James Bowling, 96
Mozley, Jemima, Newman's younger surviving sister, 30, 87, 95, 100
Munro, Miss G., 118

Napoleon, 51
Neri, *see* Philip
Newman, Francis, John Henry's brother, 20

Newman, John Henry

1. Main events of his life mentioned in this book:
Conversion experience, 13f; Oriel Fellowship, 22f; ordination as deacon in the Church of England, 24; curate at St Clement's, 24, 28; Tutorship, 28, 31; Vicar of St Mary's, 29; Illness in Sicily, 40-44, 71, 146; at Littlemore, 80ff; hears first confession, 80; resigns St Mary's, 96; joins Church of Rome, 100; becomes an Oratorian, 107; establishes Oratory in England, 110; Achilli trial, 122-5; founds Catholic University in Dublin, 119, 123, 127f, 142; becomes editor of the *Rambler*, 138; made cardinal, 181

2. Works discussed:
Apologia, 11ff, 15, 31, 47, 98, 145, 157-9, 162; *Arians of the Fourth Century*, 34; *Callista*, 113; *Certain Difficulties Felt by Anglicans in Catholic Teaching*, 116f; *Discourses to Mixed Congregations*, 113; *Dream of Gerontius*, 159-69, 180; *Essay in Aid of a Grammar of Assent*, 82f, 175-81; *Essay on the Development of Christian Doctrine*, 84, 98-100, 117; *Essay on Miracles*, 28; *Historical Sketches*, 111; *see also* Appendix; *Idea of a University*, 126; *Lectures on the Difficulties of Anglicanism*, 104; *Lectures on Justification*, 65f, 74;

Loss and Gain, 165; *Meditations on Christian Doctrine*, 148; *Oxford University Sermons*, 9, 22, ch. 3 passim; *Parochial and Plain Sermons*, 9, ch. 3 passim; *Poems*, 36, 28f; esp., 'Lead, Kindly Light', 45, and 'The Two Worlds', 146f *Sermons on Subjects of the Day* ch. 4 passim; *Tracts for the Times*, 50ff, esp. *Tract90*, 78, 85f; *Via Media*, 61.

3. His views on various subjects:
Austerity, 80; Catholic Church, 106, 145, 149, 155, 185, 189; celibacy, 19, 71; change, 118; Christ, 50-53, 96, 113, *see also* Christ in Subject Index; converts, 141f; democracy, 75; dogma, 178f; education, 28f; Eucharist and Holy Communion, 20, 22, 24, 29, 144; Evangelicalism, 14f, 16, 23ff, 27, 83; freedom (intellectual), 130f; friendship, 22, 153; God, awareness of, 176; humour, 72, 104f, 124; laity, 120, 129; Mass, 106; mystery, 35; nature, 36f; Oxford, 106; papal infallibility, 173ff pessimism, 53-56, 76; prayer and meditation, 23f, 91ff, 102, 141, 178; city of Rome, 38f; self-examination, 18f, 20ff, 41f, 91ff, 108f, 140f, 152f; spiritual direction, 81-83; trials and purification, 24, 92f, 109, 133-7, 140f, 143, 146, 148, 160

Newman, Mary, 30
Noah, 132

Norfolk, Duchess of, 181
Norfolk, Duke of, 153

Oriel College, 22f
Origen, 31, 62, 65, 126, 165f, 171

Paine, Thomas, 12
Pascal, Blaise, 82, 84, 175
Paul, St, 15, 53, 66, 111, 137, 149, 151f, 153, 179
Peel, Robert, 32
Peter, St, 52
Philip Neri, St, 107, 118, 134, 146, 154
Pindar, 27
Pius IX, 103
Plotinus, 14
Pugin, A. W. N., 118
Pusey, E. B., 27f, 32, 76, 94, 101, 132, 169ff

Rambler, 138, 140
Raphael, 167
Rogers, Frederic, 37, 41, 79f
Rose, St of Lima, 113
Rosmini, A., Rosminians, 95

Scott, Thomas, 15
Scott, Walter, 105
Stephen, St, 52
St John, Ambrose, 102, 104, 110, 143, 181

Talbot, George, 122, 138
Taylor, Jeremy, 83
Teilhard de Chardin, 63, 132
Teresa, St, of Avila, 36, 69, 148f
Teresa, St, of Lisieux, 112, 128, 150
Thackeray, William Makepeace, 105
Theodoret, 112
Thomas Aquinas, St 63, 108, 126, 129, 149, 160, 168
Thomas More, *see* More
Times, The, 87
Trent, Council of, Tridentine, 50, 85
Trinity College (Oxford), 16f
Trollope, Anthony, 105

Ullathorne, W. B., 121

Vatican Council I, 172ff, 181
Vatican Council II, 67, 118, 139, 144
Victoria, Queen, 9
Virgil, 27

Ward, William George, 159, 173, 180
Whately, John, 23
Wilberforce, H. W., 40, 125, 140
Wilberforce, Robert, 30
Wilberforce, W., 22, 30
Wiseman, Nicholas, 79, 101, 103, 107, 119, 122, 138f, 159
Wootten, Frances, 150

SUBJECT INDEX

Angel(s), 11, 17, 30, 53, 62f, 64, 72, 88, 107, 114, 163ff; guardian angel, 163ff; 'angelicals', 167f

Angst, 161

Arians, 35, 139; semi-Arians, 86

Aridity, *see* Dryness

Asceticism, 127

Baptism, baptismal regeneration, 25, 27, 64, 67

Beatific Vision, 165

Bible, *see* Scripture

Breviary, 80, 82

British Empire, 49

Calvin, Calvinism, 13f, 20, 25, 28, 47, 50, 77

Carmelites, 111

Catholic Emancipation, 31f, 48

Celibacy, 130

Certainty, 83. *See also* Doubts

Charity, *see* Love

Christ, in gen , 147, 149, 167f; the one Mediator, 67; imitation of, 73f; Heart of, 114; *see also* Newman

Church, pillar of truth, 35, a power, 89f; Church of Rome the true Church, 158f, 161

Church Fathers, 27, 30f, 34f, 37, 50, 63, 67, 77, 79, 86, 118, 163, 167, 169ff, 180

Common Prayer, Book of, 11, 50, 74f

Conscience, *see* Proofs for the existence of God

Contemplation, -ives, 102, 147, 178

Creeds, 34f, 77; pseudo-Athanasian (Quicunque), 77, 179

'Dark Night', 94, 136, 142f, 160, 162, 167

Death, 161f

Detachment, 127

Development of doctrine, 132; *see also* Newman

Devil, 41, 46, 54, 136, 164f

Dominicans, 93

Doubts and difficulties, 82f, 158, 176; *see also* Faith

Dryness, 82, 140

Education, and religion, 33, 145; dangers of, 54

Emotions, 55f, 60, 73

'Enthusiasm', 20

Eternity, 164; *see also* Time

Evangelicalism, -ists, 23, 30, 34, 37, 52, 55, 65, 73

Existence of God, *see* Proofs

Existential, -ism, 161f, 180

Faith, in gen., 41, 65, 89, 105, 118, 127, 131; confession of, 161; and difficulties, 83, 155, 158, 176; and dogma, 34; foundation of spiritual life, 171; intellectual foundations of, 174ff; and probabilities, 177; of Protestants, 116; venture, 83f, 162; and works, 15

Fastings, 72

Fathers, *see* Church Fathers

Feelings, *see* Emotions

Final perseverance, 13f

Friendship, 70-72

Fundamentalism, 51

God, *see* Proofs

Grace, 57, 65f, 99, 116f, 121, 128, 141; in schismatical Church, 80

Hebrews, Epistle to, 52, 83

Hell, 59, 94, 168f

Holiness, 31, 48, 56f, 64, 66, 68, 81f, 86, 118, 136, 150, 152f, 164; of God 50, 166; sign of the Church, 90

Holy Communion, 17; *see also* Newman

Holy Spirit, 14, 41, 65f, 173; indwelling, 63-68

Homilies, Book of, 85

Humility, 149

Ideal Christians, 68-70

Illative sense, 177f

Image of God, 35

Immaculate Conception, 138, 170

Imputed righteousness, 27

Incarnation, 98f, 119

Indulgences, 104, 108

Infallibility, in gen., 159; papal, 173ff

Intellect, *see* Reason

Invisible world, 12f, 25f, 29f, 35, 38, 41, 43f, 60-63, 114f, 158, 160, 182

Jansenism, -ist, 47, 52, 77

Jerusalem bishopric, 87

John's Gospel, 179; his First Letter, 179; the Apocalypse attributed to him, 179

Joy, 54, 60, 69, 91, 104, 152

Justification, doctrine of, 65f, 74, 77

Laity, 120f, 129f, 138, 140; *see also* Newman

Lent, 59f, 89, 91

Liberalism (religious), 29, 32f, 51f, 164

Loreto, Holy House of, 104

Love, 70f, 99, 114; and fear, 99f; and obedience, 75f

Luther, -anism, 50, 65, 77

Magdalen, Mary, 114

Mary, the Blessed Virgin, 31, 124, 133, 139, 147, 169-71; *see also* Immaculate Conception

Mass, 106

Materialism, 61

Matter, capable of sanctification, 99

Miracles, 31, 119

Modern thought, 83

Modernist controversy, 182

Moralism, -ity, 51, 55, 65

Music, 55f

Mystery, 35, 114, 158, 180

Mysticism, -ical, 66f, 100, 103, 109,

Mysticism—*continued*
160ff, 171, 175; mystical theology,
134f

Nothingness, 162
'Notoriety', 115
Novels, 54f
Novenas, 108

Obedience, 55, 58, 74-76, 143, 149,
173
Oratorians, -ory, 107; *see also* New-
man
Original Sin, 158
Oxford Movement, 9, 36, 46, 47-78

Patristics, *see* Church Fathers
Penance, 31
Perfection, ladder of, 136
Prayer, 62, 65. *See also* Newman
Prayer Book, *see* Common Prayer,
Book of
Predestination, 77
Proofs for the existence of God, 13,
84, 158, 174; from conscience, 174f
Psalms, 168; imprecatory, 50
Purgatory, 160, 165ff
Rationalism, 51
Real Presence, 31
Reason, and faith, 120, 127, 177; and
obedience, 173; and rebirth of in-
tellect 158f; and revelation, 132
Reformation, 31, 94
Relics, 119
Revelation, 98, 131f
Reverence, 52
Risk, 83ff, 89; *see also* Faith
Rome, Church of, 31
Rosary, 12, 104

Sacraments, 33, 57, 62ff, 88; of pen-
ance, 113; *see also* Newman
Saints, 28, 57, 59, 68f, 82, 91, 94, 99,
111f, 118, 136, 149f; lives of, 111f,
148; *see also* Appendix; two types,
128f
Sanctity, *see* Holiness
Satan, *see* Devil
Schoolmen, Scholastics, -ism, 84, 126,
174f, 179
Science, 63; and Church, 159; and
religion, 128, 130; and revelation,
131
Scripture, 34f, 50, 63, 74, 77, 83, 90
Senses of the soul, 65, 165
Shekinah, 66f
Sin, sinners, 47f, 50, 56-59, 60, 63,
113f, 116, 164
Spiritual senses, *see* Senses of the
soul
Stoic, -ism, 69, 152
Syllabus Errorum, 131

Te Deum, 180
Temporal power, 174
Temptation, 91, 152; *see also* New-
man
Thirty-Nine Articles, 78, 85, 156
Time, and eternity, 163; problem of,
164, 169
Tradition, 31, 180
Transcendence, 35
Transforming union, 166
Trials, *see* Temptations
Trinity, 15, 20
Truth, in gen., 157; and devotion,
132; and understanding, 131

Ultramontanes, 159, 173

Unseen world, *see* Invisible world

Veni Creator, 180
Ventures of faith, *see* Risk
Via Media, 50, 77, 79

Virgin, Blessed, *see* Mary
Virginity, 31
Virtue, 55

Wound of love, 114, 166f